Contents ✔ KU-636-355

Carol Smillie's Working Mum's Handbook

Carol Smillie's Working Mum's Handbook

Carol Smillie with Eileen Fursland

Typeset by Phoenix Photosetting, Chatham, Kent.

Printed and bound in Great Britain by
Mackays of Chatham, Chatham, Kent

This edition first published in Great Britain in 2007 by
Virgin Books Ltd
Thames Wharf Studios
Rainville Road
London
W6 9HA

First published by Virgin Books Ltd in 2003

A catalogue record for this book is available from the British Library.

ISBN 978 0 7535 1134 3

The paper used in this book is a natural, recyclable product made from
wood grown in sustainable forests. The manufacturing process conforms
to the regulations of the country of origin.

Introduction

Being a mum is probably the most complex, exhausting, emotional, difficult yet wonderful thing that has ever happened to me. If you are a mother, you'll understand what I mean. Add to that all the feelings you have about leaving your child and returning to work and you may find the whole idea of becoming a 'working mum' a little overwhelming. I know I did.

Other people seemed to be able to manage it, I thought at first. Surely it couldn't be that difficult, could it? But two months after having my first baby, I still wasn't dressed before midday, the sound of crying made me leap to my feet and going out anywhere, even just to the supermarket, was a major expedition! How on earth was I going to manage to return to work?

That first job date loomed on the horizon and brought me out in a cold sweat, forcing me to adopt the ostrich mentality – ignore it and it'll go away!

Three children later, I'm still learning and I certainly don't consider myself to be an expert but I know I've gained in confidence through sharing experiences with friends and through good old-fashioned trial and error. There are no hard and fast rules – it's just a question of finding the right solution for you and your family.

I think being a mum is a wonderful privilege but being a working mum is an art in itself and takes a certain amount of guts and stamina. Hopefully this book will give you confidence, remind you that you're not alone and help you make the most of what could be the busiest and best time of your life.

Carol Smillie

Chapter 1:
Am I doing the right thing?

Wouldn't it be great if we could be in two places at once? Imagine it: we could be at home with our children, playing or enjoying sunny walks in the park; and at the same time we could be out at work, earning money and having the satisfaction of developing our career or doing our job well.

But of course we can't do both. The rallying cry used to be 'Women can have it all!' but we are more realistic now. We know we may not be able to have it all – but we can have some of everything.

If you are reading this book, the chances are that you are planning to go back to work or are already a working mum. You have faced those difficult questions: can I manage to combine work and a family? How will it affect my child, and my relationship with him? And will I be happy?

The questions are the same for all of us, whether we are going back to work through choice or necessity, and they are the same no matter how much money we earn and where we are on the career ladder.

We are the lucky ones. Compared with fifty years ago, when mothers were not expected to work, there are now more choices open to us and many more women are able to combine motherhood and work. Equal opportunities legislation and new employment rights for parents have improved the situation for working mothers. But it doesn't mean that making those choices and decisions is always going to be easy, or that being a working mum will always be easy.

In making the decision to work, many different things come into play: our job and what it means to us; what kind of childcare we can find, or afford; our finances; our relationships; our feelings and beliefs about a mother's role.

This book includes plenty of information, ideas and suggestions that we hope will help you think through all these factors, cope with the challenges and achieve the work–life balance that is right for you and your family.

Working mums in the headlines

There's one thing you can be sure of as a mother, whether you work or not: there will be a headline along soon that will strike fear into your heart.

One minute working mums are being praised for providing their children with a positive role model; the next they are condemned for sacrificing their children's happiness on the altar of their career ambitions.

Some sections of the media delight in reporting studies which, at first glance, appear to show some harmful effect or other of mothers going out to work or of children being 'deprived' of maternal care. Equally, mums who look after their children at home have to contend with reports about the beneficial effects of nurseries or of having a working mother as a role model.

The results seem conflicting. And many of these studies are based on small samples of children that may not be representative of *your* child.

Some studies are observational, which means they can find links between childcare and certain behaviour patterns but they cannot tell us conclusively whether the childcare causes the behaviour.

Sometimes even the researchers themselves are a little startled when the results are emblazoned across the media, and they try to emphasise that more research is needed before any definite conclusions can be drawn.

You need to read media reports with a critical eye. For example, one newspaper headline recently said that scientists had discovered that having sons 'really can shorten a mother's life'. Each male child shortens the life of his mother by 34 weeks, the newspaper reported breathlessly. However, a careful reading of the rest of the article revealed that the researchers were from a university in Finland and had done their research by looking at church records of births and deaths from 1640 to 1870. So, fascinating stuff, but how relevant is it to us, here and now – and even if it was, what could we do about it?

The same questions could be asked of many of the media scare stories about the long-term effects of childcare and mothers going out to work.

When you are reading reports on childcare, it's important to bear in mind that the quality of childcare is all-important. The quality can vary – just as the quality of parenting can vary.

Much of the research comes from the US. Up to now, there has been little large-scale systematic research in the UK on the effect of early childhood education and care. Some studies come from organisations with an axe to grind, so – whether the message is good or bad – they may have put a particular spin on the report. If a report worries you, track down the original research and read it carefully before you go and snatch your child out of that nursery for fear of him becoming a juvenile delinquent. You may discover that the findings are not as inflammatory as they are reported to be.

You know *your* child and *your* child minder, nanny or nursery, so make up your own mind. You are the best judge of the quality of the care your child is getting and how well your arrangement is working.

> ### Carol says:
>
> You can tell from the children's behaviour whether you are doing the right thing or the wrong thing. It's different for everybody. No one can sit in judgment on anyone else until they've been there.

Is it worth it?

Going back to work after having a child is a new chapter in your life. Once you have a child, you will probably feel differently about work. The benefits and costs of working after you have had a baby are different from those that applied before.

Some mums find that they appreciate their job more – they are actually not that keen on being stuck at home with the baby. They like having a 'work' identity that is separate from their identity as a mother; they enjoy their work and spending their day with other adults, and they want an income of their own.

But other mothers going back to work for the first time feel impossibly torn between their job and their baby. Having a baby overturns many of your cherished beliefs and ideals. And even if you had it all carefully planned out before you became pregnant – go on maternity leave, have baby, take six months off, then take up the reins again – you may find that, when the time comes, leaving your baby is one of the hardest things you've ever done.

Carol says:

Before they have a baby, a lot of people don't understand what it's going to be like afterwards. They think: 'That's fine, I'll go back to work afterwards,' and they don't appreciate the huge pull they will feel. I have watched it in lots of friends. They can see the date is looming and they are getting themselves in a state about it, thinking, 'I don't really want to go back.' It is so hard.

It isn't only leaving a baby that is difficult. It can be just as hard when your child is a toddler, or even school-age, and wants you around all the time. What's more, older children can tell you how they feel.

Working mothers sometimes experience a painful clash of ideologies with their children – the case for equal opportunities cuts no ice with a child who just wants his mum.

Very few working mothers could say hand on heart that they had never felt guilty about leaving their children. It's something we all have to deal with in our own way. Not only when you first go back to work, but right the way through until your children are at secondary school, you are likely to feel pulled in two directions – it goes with the territory.

Being a working mother may involve some personal conflict, and leaving your children will sometimes tear at your heart-strings – but that doesn't mean you can't make a go of it or that it is 'wrong'.

You have to weigh up everyone's needs and your own situation, talk it over with your partner (if you have one), and decide what you feel comfortable with and what feels right to you.

You may feel that the people around you would disapprove of you leaving your baby and going back to work. Alternatively, perhaps your family, friends and colleagues will throw up their hands in horror if you 'sacrifice' a promising career in order to be with your children for a while. But their opinions and attitudes don't matter – it is an intensely personal decision for you and your partner to make and you have to disregard what anyone else may think.

> ### Carol says:
>
> Sometimes I and other women on television who have children get letters from viewers saying that we shouldn't be doing what we do, that we should be at home with our children. But people actually have no idea how much or how little I work. They think they do – they think that every time they see me on the television I am away from my children, but I'm not. Some of the programmes were recorded months

earlier. It is quite annoying at times, being judged by other people who don't know the full story.

I don't let it bother me, though. You'll never please all the people all the time. I know my children are happy, my husband is happy and I am happy, so that's fine. It's really nobody else's business.

Why the work balance is different once you are a mum

Apart from the emotional cost of leaving your baby or child, the high cost of childcare comes into the equation. Many mothers feel that it simply isn't worth going back to work because, after paying for childcare, they would have so little left from their wages. If you have two preschool children to pay for, the situation is even worse.

Even if you have an informal childcare arrangement, for instance with a relative or friend, which does not cost you anything, there are other costs involved: for example you may feel indebted to your mother-in-law (heaven forbid!), or you may have to look after your friend's child in return.

However, take into account your long-term earning power, even when you wouldn't be much better off financially in the short term by returning to your job. Depending on what kind of work you do, taking a break of several years could leave you at a disadvantage when you want to re-enter the labour market.

The cost of childcare has most impact on low earners. According to a 2002 survey called *Work, Parenting and Careers* by the Chartered Institute of Personnel and Development (CIPD), in households with an annual income of less than £20,000 a year, women are most likely to give up work completely. In contrast, nearly 60 per cent of higher earners – households earning over £40,000 a year – report that they are working the same number of hours.

Being able to pay for good quality, reliable childcare and perhaps even help around the house makes life easier for high-earning working mothers. On the other hand, there are some things that money can't buy, and – whatever your earning power – you may prefer to make the financial sacrifices that could enable you to give up work and be with your children while they are little.

Many women don't have much choice about going back to work. Perhaps they are on their own, and the stark choice is to live on benefits or go out to work. Or they have a partner whose income, on its own, would not cover even the basic costs of the mortgage and bills. Or they simply feel that it's essential to have some financial independence.

If you are in a position to choose whether to work or stay at home, and you are weighing up the pros and cons, try to be realistic about the challenges of each of the options.

Don't make the mistake of idealising the 'full-time mum at home' scenario. Being at home has its pleasures and its pains, just as being a working mother does. For instance, you might feel a lack of intellectual stimulation or social contact, or that you would worry more about your long-term career prospects or financial problems. And, as you'll know if you've had maternity leave, looking after a baby is no picnic. Mums who are at home full-time looking after a baby and toddler probably work harder than most people who are officially at work!

In the CIPD survey, 80 per cent of working parents said that having children had increased their stress levels either slightly or considerably. But the report added: 'Interestingly, this stress does not seem to be affected by working status:

parents working full-time experience similar stress levels to those who have given up work to raise a family.'

On the other hand, you might decide that you will be happier if you take a few years out of your working life to stay at home during your children's early years, and return to work later on. It's a bit of a cliché, but as any woman whose children are teenagers or have grown up will tell you: they are young for such a short time, and it goes so quickly.

What kind of working mum will you be?

There's no denying that being a working mum does take a lot of determination, energy and organisation – but hundreds of thousands of women do it successfully, and so can you.

There are many different ways of being a working mother. You might continue just as you did before. You might even find that you have a renewed commitment, feeling that if you have to go out to work, you want to get the maximum possible out of your job. Or you might choose what the Americans call 'the Mommy track' – you continue to work, but perhaps work fewer hours or in a less high-pressure role for a few years, in order to more easily combine your career with your family responsibilities. You might take a part-time job, so as to split your week between work and looking after your child. Or you might decide to share the child-care with your partner, each of you working shifts or part-time in order to share equally the 'family' work and the paid work.

Many women have gone back to work reluctantly – but weeks or months down the line, everything is working out fine, they are confident that their child is well cared for and they are happy with their decision.

And remember, your circumstances are not set in stone. If you decide to return to work and, after giving it a go, you are still unhappy or it's not working out, then you can reassess the situation and perhaps make changes. Chapters 2 and 12 of this book will help you.

Carol says:

At times I've felt, 'Is it worth it?' but I think we both agree that our lives are better with me working – at the moment, anyway. My job is likely to be quite short-lived – I'm not going to be a television presenter when I'm fifty or sixty, so we are enjoying it while it lasts.

Chapter 2:
Options for working mums

More and more of us are adopting working patterns that are different from the standard Monday to Friday, nine to five slog.

Some industries, like hotels, leisure and nursing, have always needed their employees to work antisocial hours. Increasingly, other businesses are keen to operate round the clock, because customers want to use their services outside normal working hours or they operate in the global marketplace, in different time zones. At the same time, new technology is making it much easier for more people to work at or from home.

And more businesses and organisations are realising that in order to attract and keep employees – and get the best out of their workforce – it is in their interests to adopt 'family-friendly' working practices. This often means offering flexible hours and a choice of working patterns, as well as other perks.

All this means there could be more options open to you if you're planning to go back to work after maternity leave or a career break. The same is true if you are already working but want to change your work patterns, or even change your job.

Whether a different working pattern would be realistic for you depends, of course, on the kind of job you have, the industry you're in, your childcare options, the hours your partner works (if you have one), how amenable your organisation is and the likely impact on your career prospects.

Career suicide?
There are still some workplaces stuck in the Dark Ages where the term 'part-timer' is an insult and women are made to feel that going part-time or working from home is career suicide.

More than 400 marketing and personnel executives earning between £30,000 and £100,000 per year were questioned for a research study by the Work–Life Balance Trust in 2002. Two-thirds said they would like to work more flexibly, perhaps by putting in some hours at home, switching to a job-share or working outside normal office hours. But eight out of ten of them believed this would ruin their promotion prospects and bring their careers to a full stop.

However, all parents with children under six now have the legal right to request more flexible hours and location of work (see 'Asking for change', later in the chapter). Let's hope that as people take advantage of this new legislation, it will bring about a shift in attitudes. Changing the culture in the workplace to make it more family-friendly is just as important as changing the policies.

Saying no to the nine to five

Here, for the record, are some of the possibilities:

⊙ Flexitime gives you more choice about your working hours, so that you can vary your start, finish and break times. You work a set number of hours, perhaps with certain agreed core times when you have to be at work.

⊙ Compressed working hours – working the same total number of hours but over a shorter number of working days – for instance full-time hours over four days a week or nine days a fortnight, giving you a regular day off.

⊙ Term-time only – you remain on a permanent contract, either full-time or part-time, but have unpaid leave during school holidays.

⊙ Working from home – you arrange to work at least part of the week from home, saving time on commuting and allowing you to work more flexibly.

⊙ Shift working or any other kind of work pattern outside the normal nine to five, for instance early mornings, late evenings, night shifts or weekend working.

Find out what's on offer

Find out whether your employers are willing to provide any form of flexible working to their staff – don't simply assume they wouldn't consider it.

A study carried out by the Joseph Rowntree Foundation in 2002 looked at staff working in six large workplaces including local government, supermarkets and retail banking. It found that, although the workplaces had adopted a wide range of family-friendly employment policies (including compassionate leave, carer's leave, flexitime, shift-swapping arrangements and voluntary reductions in hours), as many as half the employees surveyed were unaware of these options.

The moral of the story is: if you don't know, ask – and you may be pleasantly surprised.

Long hours and unusual work patterns

If you or your partner have to work early mornings or late into the evening, you're not alone.

A survey carried out in 2002 for the National Centre for Social Research found that, in most two-income families, one or both parents are working hours outside the standard 'nine to five' – including almost one in three fathers who frequently work over 48 hours a week. Fathers in professional and managerial jobs work the longest hours of all and are least likely to be involved in their children's care.

The researchers found that:

- ⊙ A fifth of mothers and four out of ten fathers worked early mornings several times a week

- ⊙ A quarter of mothers and 45 per cent of fathers regularly worked in the evening between 5.30 and 8.30 p.m.

- ⊙ One in seven mothers and one in six fathers worked night shifts several times a week

- ⊙ Almost four out of ten mothers and more than half of all fathers worked at least one Saturday a month

- ⊙ A quarter of mothers and just under a third of fathers worked at least one Sunday a month

Parents in professional jobs usually have more say in choosing working arrangements to suit their career aspirations and family needs. But parents, especially fathers, in lower socioeconomic groups have less option about working unusual hours and no scope to negotiate more flexible arrangements.

Working atypical hours works well for some families and can mean they don't need to find any formal childcare. But there are drawbacks too. Working odd hours can limit the time you spend in the evenings with your children and mean that sitting down to a family meal together is a rare event.

And couples working odd hours have even less time to spend alone together than other parents – they are like ships that pass in the night.

Part-time work/job sharing

Many women feel that this is the ideal solution to the dilemma of combining work and family. You don't give up your career alto-gether – you are still bringing in money and enjoying the other benefits of working life, like the buzz of the job and being with colleagues. Even if you drop out of the fast lane, career-wise, it will be easier to pick up speed again later on than if you had taken a complete career break. You work, yet you still have time to spend with *les enfants* and do a bit of housework, studying or just enjoy a bit of relaxation, without having to squeeze everything into just a few hours after work (when you are tired) or at weekends.

Of course, first you have to find your part-time job. In some types of work this shouldn't be too difficult, but in others part-time vacancies, especially in higher-level, well-paid jobs, are hard to find.

If you aren't seeing adverts for the kind of part-time jobs you want, it is worth considering job sharing a full-time post. You need to find a job-share partner – this may be an old colleague who is in the same boat, for instance, or someone you find through the grapevine who has similar or complementary skills. You and your job-share partner apply for the job together as a 'package' and explain the benefits of this arrangement in your application.

One recruitment company, Flexecutive (see page 170) has set up a job-sharers' register to help people (especially teachers) find suitable job-share partners to apply for jobs with. It also advises on writing a combined job-sharers' CV and runs workshops to help job sharers work together effectively.

If you are currently working full-time and you would like to do the same job part-time, see the section *Asking for change,* later in the chapter.

If you work part-time you are entitled to be treated the same as a full-time worker. So you should get, pro rata:

⊙ The same hourly rate as a full-time employee

⊙ Access to the company pension scheme and any benefits such as private health insurance

⊙ Bonus and share options

⊙ Training and career development

⊙ Paid holiday

⊙ Sick pay, maternity leave and so on

But remember – if you start to work part-time, you do not have the right to go back to full-time work later on (though an individual employer may, of course, be willing to consider this). And if you lose your job, any redundancy payments will be based on your part-time salary.

Lena says:

I job-share with another working mum – we both work two and a half days a week from Monday to Friday.

It means that, on three days a week, I can pick my son up from school. On the other days he goes to an after-school club or his dad will pick him up.

It works well for me because I get part of the week to be a stay-at-home mum and I get to have a career the other part of the week. It also means I have time to do a course to improve my IT skills.

Working from home

Some people seem to think that you can combine working at home with looking after your children. What planet are they from? Anyone who knows anything about looking after babies and toddlers will realise that, unless you are a child minder, this simply can't be done.

And don't think that getting your mum or someone else in to look after your child while you shut yourself away is going to work. You'll need a will of iron to sit at your computer and ignore what's going on beyond your door, and if your child knows you are in the house he won't rest for a minute until he has wormed his way into the room and onto your lap.

No, getting your child out of the house – whether it's to your mum's, a child minder, nursery or playgroup – is your only hope. Even then, you will have to be unbelievably single-minded in order to get on with your work and ignore the thousand and one jobs around the house that are screaming for your attention.

If your work is anything less than fascinating, chores like hanging out the washing, defrosting the fridge and renewing your car insurance suddenly become strangely attractive. You might even – heaven forbid – find yourself incapable of resisting the temptations of daytime TV.

The beauty of working from home is that you have fewer inter-ruptions from work colleagues, no ghastly commute to work, no boss breathing down your neck and no time-wasting meet-ings. You don't have to wear heels, and you can work at a time that suits you. That might mean starting work at seven-thirty in the morning and knocking off in time to collect your child from school, or having a couple of hours off to watch the school play and making up the time in the evening.

So how can you make working at home work for you?

⦿ Think about your working environment – do you have the equipment and space you need?

⦿ Keep your work space clear of anything that is likely to distract you. You need a dedicated space for your work, preferably in a room you can keep closed, so that your papers and your keyboard are safe from sticky fingers.

⦿ Your professional image will suffer if your children answer the phone, so tell them it's not allowed.

⦿ Consider installing an extra phone line so you can have one for your personal life and the other for work. You can put the 'personal' answering machine on during the day so that you don't end up chatting to your friends, and your business answering machine on after your working day is over, so that work doesn't interfere with your family time.

⊙ Some people who work at home swear by putting on work clothes and make-up, rather than comfy sweatshirt and joggers, for getting them in the right frame of mind.

⊙ You have to be disciplined with yourself. Set a start and finish time to your working day. If you say, 'I'll just make this dental appointment and book the car in for a service, then I'll start work,' before you know it an hour will have passed and you'll still be 'just loading the dishwasher' or 'just taking these toys upstairs'.

⊙ Deadlines concentrate the mind wonderfully. If your deadline is a long way ahead and you're finding it difficult to motivate yourself, set yourself mini-deadlines – for instance, making so many phone calls a day or writing a certain number of pages of the report. If you have wasted time during the day, be strict with yourself and make up the time that evening.

⊙ Working alone, it's easy to miss out on the team spirit that comes from working with other people. If you are working for an organisation, make sure you're on the list for circular e-mails, staff newsletters and so on, and arrange some face-to-face meetings so that you are not completely out of the loop.

⊙ If there's someone you get on well with, meet up socially every now and then so that she can fill you in on office goings-on. Make an effort to get to any office social functions that you can.

⊙ Keep up to date with developments in your field, especially if you are self-employed – go to conferences, join an e-mail discussion group, meet up for lunch with people in the same line of work. Networking is vital if you are working on your own.

⊙ When you work at home, the biscuit tin and the toaster are dangerously close at hand! Keep lots of fruit and low-fat snacks in the cupboards for when you get the nibbles.

Nicola says:

Since I started working from home on two days a week, I feel much less hassled. The hours that I save on travelling to the office each day can now be spent working, so I can be flexible about things like dental appointments and school assemblies. I can go to the supermarket in the afternoon and work in the evening to make up the time. I'm much more focused as I don't get involved in office politics and unnecessary meetings. I've saved myself a lot of time and stress.

Be your own boss

You may do the kind of work where you could go it alone as a freelance or you might even have a yen to start your own business. Having a baby could be the spur that you need to strike out on your own. But all the points above about working at home still apply. And there's an extra dimension: bringing in the business.

When you work for an organisation, unless you are in a sales role, you may never have had the pressure of finding customers before. But if you are self-employed, whether as an illustrator, writer, IT consultant, trainer or whatever, it's up to you to find the commissions and assignments. Don't underestimate the amount of time (and money) you will need to spend marketing your services, as well as actually doing the work. You'll have to pay tax on your earnings – and you will still have to pay for childcare.

You also sacrifice job security, a company pension (you'll need to set up arrangements of your own), paid holidays, training and the career progression that you probably took for granted in a large company. You're likely to have peaks and troughs in your workload. There may be times when your cash flow is distinctly dodgy. And even if you already feel you have enough work on your plate, it can be hard to say 'no' to another assignment if you're afraid they may not ask you again.

But against these pitfalls you can set the job satisfaction, the increased flexibility, the sense of control that comes from being your own boss, and the fact that you are making money for yourself and your family, not the company.

The idea of going it alone can be appealing, especially once you have children. But whether you want to freelance or have ambitious plans to set up a company that will grow and employ other people, be prepared for plenty of hard work.

You'll need to think about researching the market, writing a business plan, possibly finding premises, marketing and advertising your services, book-keeping and loads of other stuff.

The good news is that there's plenty of advice and information out there about starting up and managing a business:

⊙ Look for courses called things like Women into Enterprise or Women in Business at your local further education college.

⊙ Businesslink is a national network of business advice centres provided by the government's Small Business Service, providing help and advice on every aspect of starting a business. Call 0845 600 9006 or see the website www.businesslink.org to find your nearest Businesslink.

⊙ Contact your local Enterprise Agency to find out what other help is on offer near you.

⊙ Another good starting point is the learndirect website (www. learndirect.org.uk) where you can find information on a wide variety of issues to do with starting a business and also find out about courses.

Being your own boss may be satisfying but be warned – it can be hard to keep boundaries between your working time and your family life. One female entrepreneur who won a 'Women of Achievement' award was featured in a newspaper article. The writer of the article seemed impressed by the fact that, while the Woman of Achievement was on holiday for the first time in two years, she 'was able to watch her husband and daughter on the beach, while handling urgent company business on her laptop in their seaside apartment'. Doesn't sound like much of a holiday, does it?

Direct selling

Some women are making big bucks from direct selling. The list of things you could sell includes cosmetics, fragrances, skincare, jewellery, clothes, diet plans, home-care products, books, toys and games. You sell direct to your customers, for instance through parties or by leaving your products at a playgroup or in an office. Alternatively you deliver your catalogue to potential customers and call back for their orders.

If you are an outgoing type and the idea of being a saleswoman appeals, then for a modest initial investment this could give you the opportunity to work as many or as few hours as you want, at times that suit you.

For more information, contact the Direct Selling Association (see page 170).

What about a franchise?

A franchise allows you to be your own boss but with the benefits of working under an established trade name, with support and backup from the parent company. There are hundreds of business franchises. You could run an agency supplying cleaning staff, a chocolate or doughnut shop, or even a mobile pet-care service, to name but a few.

You have to put money upfront to buy the franchise. But according to the British Franchise Association (details on page 169), 96 per cent of franchises are still in profit after five years, compared with only 45 per cent of other independent small firms.

Carol says:

Ideally you want to arrange your working life so that the job doesn't consume you completely and you still get time with your children. For me, that's weekends, and at quieter times of the year I get two or three days a week when I'm not working.

At certain times of the year I spend quite a lot of time away from the children, but I don't have a regular Monday to Friday, nine to five job. When I am filming travel programmes the work is in short, sharp bursts so I go away maybe two nights a week for about five weeks. I am conscious of not picking work that takes me away from home too much.

With the *Holiday* programme, I ended up stopping because I thought that five days away from home for five minutes on the screen was not worth it – I didn't want to be famous that badly.

Everyone said to me: 'How could you even think about giving it up?'

It's a wonderful job if you are single, unattached and have no ties – but I just thought, 'I'm not enjoying this.' Even now that the children are older, I wouldn't want to go away for that length of time.

Asking for change

If you are hoping to persuade your organisation to let you change your hours, you need to do some careful preparation beforehand.

If you are hoping to alter your working hours when you go back after your maternity leave, approach your boss as soon as you can. Don't wait until you have returned to work.

Under new legislation that came into force in April 2003, if you have a child under 6 (or a disabled child under 18) and have been working for your employer for 26 weeks, you have a legal right to request a change to your hours, to the times you are required to work or to work from home, to enable you to care for your child. Your employer is obliged to consider your request seriously and meet with you to discuss it within 28 days. Employers do not have to agree to your request for family-friendly working arrangements but if they turn it down, they have to provide clear business reasons.

Here's how to make your case:

⊙ Decide in advance what changes you would ideally like, whether this is reduced hours, job-sharing, working one day a week from home or whatever. Work out how this would affect your pay (if at all) and whether you could still manage. You can only make an application for a *permanent* change to your terms of employment.

⊙ Decide what your bottom line will be – there may be some issues where you can meet your boss halfway and others that you really do not want to budge on.

⊙ Think about the duties and responsibilities of your job and how the new arrangement could be put into practice. Look at it from your employer's point of view. Who would cover the rest of the work? What would your employer have to do, for instance would someone else need to be recruited to job-share with you? Would you have to be provided with equipment to use at home?

⊙ If you are hoping to job-share or do some work from home, communication will be a big issue. How would you communicate with your job-share partner? If you are in a senior position, would you be willing to be contacted in an emergency even if it is one of your days off?

⊙ Anticipate what your boss's objections might be – for instance, 'the job is too senior', 'it would cost too much money' or 'we wouldn't have the continuity we need' – and work out ways to counter them if you feel they are unjustified.

⊙ Ask your manager to schedule a meeting.

⊙ Write down your proposals.

⊙ Explain your reasons for wanting to change your hours – for instance to fit in with available childcare – and bear in mind that your boss is likely to react more favourably if you seem to be requesting, rather than demanding, a change.

⊙ If you think it would help, show your boss why flexible working makes good business sense in terms of improved productivity. Present some examples of other departments or similar companies where your proposed arrangement has worked well, and even saved the company money. There may be other people in your organisation who are already job-sharing, or you might be able to explain how a similar company has successfully introduced flexitime for its employees.

⊙ Several of the organisations listed on page 169, such as Working Families, New Ways to Work and the Department of Trade and Industry, can help you make your case by providing information and/or case studies.

⊙ Be prepared to be flexible and compromise – you may not get everything you want, but something is better than nothing.

⊙ Are there any other ways of achieving what you want? For instance, if your boss says no to part-time working, he or she might agree to you taking unpaid parental leave on one day a week for a fixed period.

⊙ If your boss puts a different proposal to you, you don't have to decide there and then whether to accept it – you can ask for time to give it some thought. Don't agree to anything you will regret later, like squeezing five days' work into three days.

⊙ Remember, in all negotiation, you should try to reach a win–win situation. Both sides should end up feeling that they have gained something and be satisfied with the outcome, or at least feel that they can live with it.

⊙ Although this is important to you, it's unlikely to be at the top of your boss's priority list. Give your boss plenty of time to consider.

⊙ If the answer is definitely no, try to keep your cool and not lose your temper or fall out with your boss over it – remember, for the time being at least, you still need this job.

⊙ If you believe, later on, that you have been sidelined or your promotion prospects have suffered as a result of your request, make a formal complaint.

⊙ If the answer is yes, congratulations! You will need to explain your new working hours and structure to your colleagues and make sure they know what is going on, when you are available and how to contact you. If you make it clear that you will do your best to cover for your colleagues in an emergency, you should find that they will do the same for you.

'I don't want to go out to work any more!'

Confucius said: 'Choose a job you love, and you will never have to work a day in your life.'

But in a job you don't enjoy, the days seem to drag and you walk round with a black cloud hovering over your head.

If you are desperate to give up your job and stay at home but you still need to earn just a little extra money to keep the wolf from the door, all is not lost. It may not be your dream job, but chances are you can find a way to make a bit of extra money while working fewer or more flexible hours. Think about some of these:

⊙ Could you do whatever it is that you do from home? For instance, if you are a teacher, you could do home tuition. See the section on working from home, above.

⊙ Could you find a local job working evenings or weekends only, so that you could spend your days with your child and leave him with your partner or a relative while you work?

⊙ You could make money by direct selling (see above) in the evenings or while your child is at playgroup.

⊙ If you live in a tourist area and have a spare room or two, you could run your own bed and breakfast. Find out more from the English Tourist Board, Thames Tower, Black's Road, London W6 9EL – it has some helpful publications including *Starting a Bed and Breakfast Business*.

⊙ If you live in a town or city and have a spare room in your house, what about taking a lodger? You could let the room to a business person, visiting academic or young teacher.

⊙ You could become a child minder and combine looking after other people's children with looking after your own. It's hard work but if you looked after several children you could earn a decent wage. For more information, contact the National Childminding Association, details on page 173.

⊙ If you are artistically minded, could you make and sell a product? For instance, you could make a bit of profit from something like hand-made greetings cards or gifts if you find the right up-market outlets to sell them.

⊙ Is there a service you can offer to people – dressmaking, gardening, word-processing? You won't make a fortune, but you might just make enough to make it possible for you to give up your current job.

⊙ Beware 'get-rich-quick' schemes that promise a fortune to homeworkers – they usually turn out to be a scam.

Chapter 3:
Going back to work

When Liz Hurley turned up for her first photo session five months after giving birth to her son Damian, the magazine editor was amazed.

'Her nails were done, her legs were waxed. She was totally ready for work. Her appearance and her behaviour were immaculate,' she is reported as saying. 'In two days of very hard work she never once did anything that wasn't charming or polite ... There was no grubbiness. Her underwear was immaculate ...'

Apparently she even kept the telephone calls to a minimum.

Liz was only doing what thousands of other new mums do when it comes to returning to work (with slightly less emphasis on the underwear) – showing that they are going to do their damnedest to make a success of it.

Perhaps you've been dreading your return to work, or perhaps it can't come soon enough for you. You may hate the whole idea of leaving your child, or maybe you are desperate to be a working woman again. You might be leaving your baby for the first time – or looking for a new job after a long career break, two or three children down the line.

Whether you are returning through choice or necessity, whatever your situation, in this section you'll find some tips here to help you with the challenge that lies ahead.

When your maternity leave is over

The hardest thing about going back after maternity leave, especially if it's your first baby, is that you feel almost like a different person. You've been through so much since your colleagues waved you off with good-luck cards and presents for your baby-to-be.

You have given birth and there's now another little human being who depends on you – an experience that transforms your life so utterly and completely, in such a short time, that you feel as though the whole world must have changed. Some of the things that used to matter so much to you now seem irrelevant. You are at the mercy of profound and powerful new feelings and your priorities may be very different from before.

But, back at your workplace, your colleagues are likely to be oblivious to all of this. While your world was changing, theirs has continued much as before. In fact, it's been said of women who work in the City that their bosses would be a lot more understanding if they came out as a cocaine addict rather than a new mother.

When you start back at work, you might indeed find that the company's monthly sales targets somehow don't seem quite as compelling as before. Or you might be determined that, even though you're now a mother, you will be just as committed to your career as you ever were.

Whatever your feelings – or the attitudes of people around you – somehow you have to find a way to get back in the swing.

Smoothing the way to a successful return to work starts well before your first day back. Keeping in touch with work while you are on maternity leave helps. So does putting plans in place, where you can, that will help you feel more confident about going back.

Ideally, you will have been thinking for a while now about a number of issues that will affect your quality of life as a working mother: childcare, sleep, getting help from your partner or people around you, and taking care of yourself. The other chapters in this book should help you with these.

Carol says:

Sometimes time away from children can bring out the best in you. When you've been doing nothing but watch *Thomas the*

Tank Engine and going goo-goo all day, to have some adult conversation is quite exhilarating.

You think, 'Wow, I can put some smart clothes on!'

After I'd been at home for a while after having Robbie and then Jodie, Christie didn't recognise me when I first put working clothes on, because she hadn't seen me like that for so long. I felt like a million dollars for putting on some smart clothes and make-up.

The early days

Inevitably, your first few days back will be dominated by thoughts of your baby. You might even be the kind of new mum (lots of us are) who blubs all the way to work and phones the child minder every hour on the hour just to find out what your baby is doing now.

On your first day, even if you are crying inside, try to put on a brave face – your boss will want to hear that you are looking forward to getting on with the job.

Recognise that it will take you a little time to get back into work mode, to feel involved with what's going on in the office and to accept that your baby is fine without you. You will still miss him, of course – but it will get easier in time.

Tiredness is often a big factor too. Looking after a new baby is so exhausting that you might think going back to work will feel like a rest cure. But don't underestimate how tiring work will be at first – you'll be expending a lot of nervous energy when you first go back. You are combining a working day with looking after your baby or child in the evenings, all the usual household chores and perhaps trying to cope with broken nights at the same time. It's a lot more than you did before you had the baby.

Have early nights as often as you can, even if it means going to bed at the same time as your baby.

If you have been breast-feeding your baby (see below), be prepared in case you leak some breast milk during the day. Wear breast pads, keep some spare ones at work, and have a spare bra and top in your desk drawer as well, just in case.

If you are worried about how you'll cope, maybe you could negotiate a short period of reduced working hours so you can ease yourself in gently in the first few weeks. And be careful not to take on too many commitments at first, even if you feel you have something to prove.

If you do make mistakes or have a disaster at work, don't beat yourself up over it. Instead of saying to yourself, 'I must be useless', try to put it behind you. Everyone makes mistakes sometimes.

After work, try to switch off and forget about work so you can enjoy the time you have with your baby – don't waste it by fretting about reports and deadlines.

Penny says:

On my first day, my manager left a postcard on my desk with the words, 'I wanted to go out and change the world, but I couldn't find a babysitter.' For me, it summed up the predicament of being a working parent.

Combining work and breast-feeding

You don't necessarily have to stop breast-feeding unless you want to.

⊙ You can continue to breast-feed in the morning and evening, while your baby's carer replaces the daytime feeds with formula milk. To give your body time to adjust, drop the daytime feeds gradually, one at a time with several days in between, before you go back. Your milk supply will reduce but you will probably find you can still enjoy giving your baby the first and last feeds of the day for quite a while. Make sure your baby is used to drinking from a bottle, cup or spoon before you go back to work – talk to your health visitor about this if you are having problems.

⊙ If you're lucky enough to have a workplace crèche or child minder close to where you work and you have the kind of job where you can slip out for short periods, you may be able to visit your baby during your breaks or lunch hour to breast-feed. (That's assuming he co-operates by being awake and hungry at the right time.)

⊙ You could express breast milk while you are at work so that you have a supply of milk for your child's carer to give him. Your employer should provide a suitable place for you to express – which does not mean the ladies' loo. You will need to learn in advance how to express milk (using a pump), have a private place at work where you can relax, a fridge to store the milk in, facilities to wash and sterilise your equipment and a cool bag to take the milk home. It also helps to have understanding and supportive colleagues (unlike those who reportedly shouted 'moo' down the corridor after one new mum as she went off to express milk).

⊙ If you plan to feed your baby or express during working hours, write to your employer before you go back to work and tell him what you will need in order to do this.

⊙ Expressing milk at work can be quite a time-consuming option and you will need to be determined. There's lots of good advice on offer on the practicalities, equipment, negotiating with your employer and your legal rights as a breast-feeding mother. For instance, see *Breastfeeding: how to express and store your milk* from the National Childbirth Trust (£2.50 – see page 173 for addresses). You can hire an electric breast pump from La Leche League (see page 171) or the National Childbirth Trust (see page 173).

⊙ If you need some advice on how to manage breast-feeding and your return to work, or someone to give you moral support, a breast-feeding counsellor could help – these are volunteers, other mothers who are well informed about all aspects of breast-feeding. Contact the National Childbirth Trust or La Leche League (see page 171).

Carol says:

I had agreed to present the Scottish BAFTA awards two weeks after Robbie was born, and with hindsight it was too soon. I was still trying to breast-feed and I remember standing in the dressing room with a breast pump, thinking: 'This is a nightmare!'

I had loads of padding inside my dress in case I leaked.

I told my husband Alex, who was sitting in the audience, to give me the nod if there was a major problem that I couldn't see – although it would probably be better if I didn't know!

That was also my first big bout of mastitis – everyone else was having a wonderful time at the after-show party, while I was lying on my bed, moaning.

I carried on breast-feeding each of my children for as long as I could, but it wasn't long. I tried cabbage leaves, nipple shields and everything – I really tried but I just couldn't manage it.

I breast-fed my youngest, Jodie, for longest – six weeks – so I did get better at it!

You and your colleagues

Let's face it, one of the best things about going back to work is being with grown-ups again rather than spending all day with people under three feet tall who spit out their food and fly into uncontrollable tantrums with little warning.

Lots of mums really enjoy being part of a team again, sharing ideas and having a laugh. But for others, difficult colleagues are the most stressful part of being at work.

You may have some work colleagues who haven't got children, have no idea what you are going through and say things which you find upsetting. And that's on top of the normal irritations that can arise all the time when people work together.

Take a deep breath and get away from the person for a while to give yourself chance to calm down. Go and make a cup of coffee, go to the loo or have a walk round. When tempers have cooled, sit down with the person and discuss whatever it is that's been causing the problem. And remember, after a row, bearing a grudge is stressful – the best policy is to forgive and move on.

When there's a long-running problem or disagreement about who's responsible for what, or if you feel you are being unfairly blamed or criticised for something, ignoring it won't make it go away. You will feel resentful and your working relationships will suffer. Sometimes it's best to be upfront and stand up for yourself – without blaming other people and getting embroiled in office politics.

Linda says:

When I had my first child I was only at home four months but I couldn't believe the patronising attitudes I was subjected to when I went back. I'd been a personnel manager for five years and all of a sudden I was being talked down to by all and sundry.

Learning to love technology

With a mobile phone and a laptop you need never be out of touch with the office for a second – but the downside is that you never escape from the pressure.

These days we all suffer from information overload. Try to organise your day so that you have set periods when you deal with incoming information. E-mails are so quick and easy to send that people often produce a piece of information and mindlessly send it to everyone. If you find that you are being swamped with unnecessary circular e-mails at work, see if you can get your name taken off the address lists.

When you return to work, don't be afraid to ask for help, training or support if necessary. Being unfamiliar with a program or piece of equipment is not a sign of weakness.

Not knowing how to use the systems properly can be stressful, as one secretary found, a week into her new job. She had intended to e-mail the administration manager to let her know that the department had run out of biscuits, but inadvertently put her message on the emergency e-mail channel and sent it to the entire company. That included the managing director, who couldn't understand why the new employee was demanding that he provide her with biscuits as a matter of such urgency.

The long-hours culture

In some workplaces, managers work long hours and expect everyone else to do the same. People feel obliged to stay late to prove their commitment, to show they are indispensable or just because of peer pressure. It can be extremely difficult to be the one person in the office who leaves on time.

But it's now well recognised that the 'long-hours culture' is damaging to family life and to people's health and wellbeing. And you are likely to start resenting your job if you feel you have to work unreasonably long hours which eat into your evenings and even weekends, depriving you of precious time with your child and partner.

Yes, you are important to your employer and committed to your job, but you are important to your child too. If you feel you are being pulled in opposite directions, unable to perform either of your roles properly, just consider:

- ⊙ You are not in the wrong – the organisation is. A forward-thinking company would not demand long hours from its employees. It is uneconomic and irrational, leading to increased sickness absence, low morale, lower productivity and quality of work and higher staff turnover.

- ⊙ If everyone is working long hours as a way of life, either the workload is too heavy or the number of staff too few. This is your employer's problem and one that they should deal with.

- ⊙ If you know that you have put in a good day's work, leave on time with a clear conscience. Make it clear in a firm but friendly way that you are not going to stay late every night any more, although you will do what you can to help in an emergency.

- ⊙ With a child come new responsibilities. Apart from being desperate to see your child at the end of the day, you now have 'employees' of your own to consider, such as your child minder or nanny, and you have a duty to them to be back on time.

- ⊙ Can you be proactive about changing things in your workplace? Perhaps you could suggest that meetings take place in the morning rather than at the end of the day – that way, if they overrun, you won't all have to stay late at work.

- ⊙ Or, ask if you could arrange for the staff and managers to get together to identify the reasons why people in your company are working long hours and generate some solutions.

Commuting

You may have to leave on time at the end of the day, but make sure you're not arriving late too often as well. Everyone gets delayed sometimes, of course, but if it becomes a habit, you are laying yourself open for colleagues to point the finger. Allow plenty of time in the morning for possible cancelled trains and other hold-ups.

Sitting on the train or in traffic jams for long periods feels like a frustrating waste of precious minutes. Like working mums everywhere, you will soon find yourself making good use of this time by compiling lists of all the things you need to do just as soon as you get off the train or out of the car.

If you use your car to commute to work, protect yourself against stress by joining a breakdown service – and program the number into the memory of your mobile phone. If you can, go for the 'breakdown at home' option as well – so that on those awful mornings when your car won't even start, you can summon a wonderful man to your aid with one quick phone call.

Carol says:

When you go out to work, it's funny how the mundane things like school runs seem so much more exciting. Sometimes I really wish I was doing it – but I know that if I had to do it day in, day out, it would lose its appeal.

Often I come home exhausted after flying back from London to Glasgow and the children are already in bed asleep. I go into their rooms and look at their gorgeous little faces and think, 'Aaaaah' – and my husband will say, 'They've been horrors!'

If your employer isn't playing fair

Some employers try it on, altering a woman's job when she comes back from maternity leave. Hopefully this will never happen to you, but if it does you should take the following steps:

⊙ Tell your employer that you are not happy about the job you have been given. If you continue to do the new job while negotiating with your boss, make it clear that you are doing the work 'under protest'. Put this in writing and keep a copy for yourself.

⊙ Get as much help as possible, for instance from your union representative, staff association or a law centre or advice agency such as the Citizens' Advice Bureau. Use any grievance procedures that are in place where you work (these should be set out in your contract or staff handbook).

⊙ If you can't resolve it and you are so unhappy with your situation that you feel you have no option but to resign, get advice before you actually hand in your resignation. You could claim unfair dismissal and sex discrimination based on your constructive dismissal because of the way you have been treated, but you need to make a claim within three months. The three months' time limit could run from the date you were first told about the new job, so don't delay. Working Families can advise you (see contact details on page 177).

Getting a job after a career break

So you've decided the time has come to find a 'proper' job – but getting a foot back in the door after you've been out of the work-place for a couple of years or more can seem a daunting task. You can feel de-skilled, lacking in confidence and distinctly mumsy compared to the career women you see everywhere you look. But don't worry – you can rejoin their ranks.

The Women Returners' Network surveyed 214 women on career breaks. The main barriers the women perceived were the speed with which the demands of work are changing, a demand for higher qualifications and a feeling that people are expected to work longer hours. The main strengths they perceived they had were essentially related to their attitude and behaviour, especially the ability to cope with pressure and people. The main perceived weaknesses are the demands and distractions imposed by the need to find childcare and having to take time off work at short notice to cope with family-related emergencies.

Your route back to work

⊙ If you haven't been keeping up to date with what's going on in your line of work, now is the time to begin. Start reading the relevant journals, researching company information, maybe attending conferences, and finding out about the current issues and what the job market is like out there.

⊙ Start networking! (See below)

⊙ Do you need to upgrade your skills? Find out about refresher courses or do a course to equip yourself with the skills that are in demand now.

⊙ Learndirect (see address on page 172) provides advice on learning, whether you want to brush up your old skills or get qualified for something completely different. You can chat over the phone with a personal learning adviser who can tell you about requirements for different jobs, point you to the right course locally and tell you whether you might be eligible for help with childcare costs. You can study at home on the Internet or in a college or learning centre near you.

⊙ There are many courses and workshops around for women returners – often called 'New Directions', 'New Opportunities' or something similar. These will give you advice on job-hunting, writing your CV, interview techniques, confidence-building and so on. Ask at your local colleges and university or phone Learndirect or the Women Returners' Network (see page 177).

⊙ Borrow or buy books for women returners. The Women Returners' Network produces a workbook called *Returning to Work* (available for £5) that aims to help women identify what they have to offer employers, decide what sort of work or training they want to do, and plan their next steps.

⊙ Do some research into the kind of CV employers are looking for nowadays – there are lots of books and advice around on this. Things may have changed since you last wrote a CV – for instance, CVs are often submitted via e-mail now, and more and more companies are turning to CV-scanning equipment and software to weed through their stacks of CVs.

⊙ Start working on your own CV. The standard advice for women who have been at home looking after children is to identify your 'transferable skills'. These are the key qualities that employers are looking for, such as teamwork, communication and time management. Women are said to be particularly good at 'multitasking' too. You have been busily developing these skills, without even realising it, while running the school summer fete, masterminding the Brownie camp holiday, overseeing builders working on your extension or loft conversion and learning from your many other life experiences.

⊙ One common mistake people make on their CVs is focusing on themselves and their needs, rather than on what a prospective employer is looking for. The recruiter has his own problems. He doesn't care whether you are looking for a way to utilise your skills and advance your career – he just wants to find someone who can do this particular job and help him meet his goals.

⊙ Work out what it would take to make you feel more confident, and go for it – whether that means losing weight, taking an evening class in assertiveness or simply splashing out on a new interview suit, a pair of killer heels and a set of false nails.

⊙ Use your existing contacts as well as building new ones. Get in touch with your old company – you never know, there might be a vacancy coming up which could be the easiest way to kick-start your new career.

⊙ Plan your job search carefully. As well as advertised jobs and recruitment agencies, you can research and target specific companies that you would like to work for, even if they haven't advertised any vacancies. See 'Asking for advice' below.

⊙ If you do have unsuccessful interviews, the rejection can be hard to take. Ask for feedback so you understand why you didn't get the job. Try to see even an unsuccessful interview as a useful experience, from which you can take something to help you perform better next time.

Volunteering

The Women Returners' Network researched women in professional-grade jobs who had taken career breaks. The women were asked about any unpaid activities they had undertaken in their breaks, including various kinds of voluntary work, and the different skills these had engendered. These included people skills, negotiating, public speaking, assertiveness, minute-taking and administrative skills, bookkeeping, marketing, campaigning, keeping one's brain alert and open to new thinking, communication skills, manual skills, planning and organising, financial skills, record-keeping skills, teaching/coaching skills and IT skills.

Volunteering gives you the opportunity to use your skills or develop new ones, boosts your confidence if you have been at home with children, and enhances your CV. If it's a long time since you worked, your voluntary-work manager can act as a referee for you when you are applying for jobs. And volunteering can sometimes lead, indirectly, to paid work.

Taking on voluntary work doesn't just mean serving in a charity shop. Many voluntary organisations offer valuable training, for instance in listening and communication skills to help you support people who have been bereaved or the victims of crime, or in IT if you are volunteering in the office.

Some organisations, such as the Citizens' Advice Bureau, offer extensive training in advice and information work and demand a high degree of commitment. Other volunteering opportunities need only take an hour or so of your time each week.

Giving time helps other people as well as giving you the opportunity to get out of the house and do something different.

Many charities welcome people with business skills to join their management committees. A management committee is a group of people who lead and direct the charity, help it to achieve its aims through their expertise and commitment, and oversee its work and its finances.

If you have finance, legal, IT, marketing or human resources skills, for instance, you would have a lot to offer. However, it is quite a responsibility and demands time and effort on your part because effectively you are on the charity's board of directors. If this is too much commitment for you at the moment, you could offer your services in organising events, fundraising, publicity or some other project.

Alternatively, you could take on a role such as a school governor, a magistrate or a mentor, or help run a residents' association.

Find out about local possibilities by contacting your local volunteer bureau (to find it, look in the phone book, ask at the library or go to the website www.do-it.org.uk).

Experience counts

There's no getting round the fact that employers like candidates with recent experience; so if you've had a career break, how can you get it? As described above, voluntary work is an excellent way to get experience of work in a wide range of settings. Other possibilities are:

⊙ Think about temping or taking on short-term contracts to start with – it gets you recent experience on your CV and you can make some contacts which could well lead to a permanent job.

⊙ Look into local courses for women returners. Some of them, especially those aimed at women returning to management, include a work placement, which can be invaluable in building your confidence.

⊙ If you've been out of the workplace for a while, you may have to compromise and take a job at a slightly lower grade than the one you left. At least it gets you in from the cold and you can use the job as a springboard to greater things.

Recruitment agencies

Find a recruitment consultant who understands what you can offer and who will market you in the right way. Register with a maximum of three good companies that specialise in your field. A good recruitment company should give you a structured interview lasting at least an hour.

An interview with a recruitment consultant is different from a job interview. To some extent you can afford to come clean about gaps in your experience or potential weaknesses, so that the consultant can advise you. Think about the kind of role that would suit you and the kind of culture you work best in.

Remember, when you get a job offer, you still need to think carefully about whether this is the right job for you.

Asking for advice

The 'information interview' is a technique popular in the United States, and it's starting to catch on here too. You approach managing directors, sales directors and so on in the industry you want to work in and ask if they can spare twenty minutes or half an hour to give you advice in your search for work.

You are not asking for a job. You are telling the person about your goals and asking for guidance, and you have three aims: gaining valuable information about the organisation and/or the industry and likely opportunities; making useful contacts; and making sure that person will think of you if a job arises in the future. Unlike a job interview, you'll be asking most of the questions.

If you can't go by the 'warm' route, via a friend or associate, you'll need to research the right person. Keep your letter short, with no CV. Say that you are seeking information and ask if they would be prepared to share their knowledge and experience with you. Chances are they will be flattered and agree – at worst, they will just say that they can't spare the time.

Making such a call, when you are not representing an organisation but just yourself, is extremely daunting. But remember, you are good at what you do – and you want to find the best place to take your skills.

Use your professional association

If there is a professional association for the line of work you're in, it can keep you in the loop. As well as running seminars and conferences, it can advise you about updating your skills or finding a mentor or other contacts, and help when you are researching the job market.

Make networking work for you

Networking is all about making contact with people, keeping in touch, being better informed, exchanging ideas. It can be informal, through a company grapevine or through friends. Or it can be formal, where people from different backgrounds come together at courses, conferences and so on.

Personal contacts are invaluable in terms of finding a job or developing your career. You could make contact with someone who knows of an unadvertised vacancy, who can refer you to other useful contacts, who could be a mentor for you in a new job or even agree to coach you in a specific skill.

If you are at a suitable event, get stuck in!

⊙ Circulate, introduce yourself, find out what other people do. If you feel shy, remember that most other people will be feeling the same.

⊙ Have something in mind that you are particularly interested in, and make a point of asking people about it.

⊙ Hand out business cards. If you don't have a card from your organisation, have some printed yourself. Exchanging cards also helps if you have a bad memory for names. When someone gives you a card, note on the back of it where you met and what you discussed.

⊙ Maintain contact with people you meet, so that they will remember you.

⊙ If you can, share information or contacts with the people you meet at networking events or help them in some way. Then, when you need something, you won't have any hesitation about asking for help. That's what networking is all about.

Interviews

We don't have room in this book to discuss interview techniques, and there's plenty of information out there. So let's just look at three of the questions your interviewers might put to you.

You may be asked: 'What do you like doing in your free time?' Resist the temptation to give a hollow laugh at the very idea of 'free time' or to detail all the household/child/husband-related tasks that fill your every waking moment. Don't even talk about how much you love to relax in your free time with your adorable family, or the interviewer may get the idea that your heart would not really be in the job. As for what you *should* claim to do with your mythical free time – who knows? I'm sure you can make up something plausible.

The same goes for: 'Which achievement are you most proud of?' It might be that your finest moment was getting through the birth with only gas and air, but try to come up with something that involves skills rather more relevant to the post you are applying for.

Finally, what if your interviewer asks you if you have children, or if you plan to have any (or any more). In fact, they are not allowed to do this by law. They should ask only questions which relate to the job. However, if you *are* asked a question like this and you tell the interviewer that he has no right to ask or that it's none of his business, you might find the interview turns a little frosty. If you really want this position, answer honestly – but explain why you will still be able to do a good job.

Penny Vatkovsky from Enfield, Middlesex, has a six-year-old son called Luke. She has been working full-time as an adult guidance worker since Luke was three.

A big issue for me when I first started my job was confidence. I had recently become a single parent and part of me was terrified that I wouldn't be able to cope with working full-time.

I used to sit in meetings convinced that I shouldn't really be there. I imagined that, at some point, a very professional person who hadn't been off for years bringing up kids would find out I was really an impostor who should be attending a mother-and-toddler meeting instead of a funding meeting!

My confidence returned in time, though, and I realised that I was just as worthy of being there as anyone else and that I could do just as good a job as the next person.

Guilt was another big issue for me. I once caught myself telling the school secretary that my son couldn't possibly have a chickenpox rash because I was about to go into a meeting. Another time I forgot that it was a fancy-dress day at school and had to rush home to grab a sheet to turn Luke into a ghost. And just last week I was already at work by the time I realised it was a 'non-uniform' day at Luke's school and I immediately had to start phoning around to arrange for someone else to deliver a pair of jeans to the school for him to change into.

Perhaps my worst moment was seeing a smiling woman at the school gates on one of the rare occasions when I could take him in, and asking who her son was – only to be told that she was actually the head teacher.

It's the stuff nightmares are made of. But I've now decided that it is exactly those things that make you a good parent/employee – the fact that you are able to improvise so expertly and that, despite thinking it's impossible, you still *manage* to come up with a solution somehow.

Chapter 4:
Childcare

Finding childcare you are happy with is the most important task you face when you are contemplating returning to work, whether you are going straight back after maternity leave or have had a longer career break.

The cost of childcare is also likely to be one of your biggest outgoings in the next few years. In some areas there is a chronic shortage of childcare places, which pushes up the costs and makes for long waiting lists. Help with the cost of certain types of childcare is available for many families – see the section on tax credits on page 113.

It can be a struggle for some parents to find quality childcare or to afford to pay for it – which is why only 13 per cent of parents with dependent children use formal childcare services all the time. Many rely on informal childcare by relatives or friends, or use a mixture of different types of childcare.

In our 24-hour society there's a growing trend for couples to cope with childcare by 'shift parenting' – dovetailing their working hours so that there is always one of them at home.

The phases of childcare

The kind of childcare that you will be looking for is likely to depend on how old your child is when you go back to work. A baby or toddler has different needs from a three-year-old.

And just when you think you've got it sussed, everything changes. When your child goes to school you save money on childcare but then you have to find someone to look after him before and after school and in the school holidays.

Choosing the right option for you

There are five steps to work through, and the sooner you start, the better. You'll have more choice – a popular nursery may have a long waiting list.

1. Work out what you want (if you're on maternity leave, start doing this before your baby is born):

   ⊙ Think about the type of childcare that would work best for you and your child, bearing in mind his age and stage of development.

   ⊙ Work out how many hours of childcare you need each week and how much you can afford to pay.

   ⊙ Think about how much flexibility you are likely to need, in terms of working late or unusual hours, and how understanding your employer is likely to be if you have a childcare emergency.

   ⊙ Decide how far you would realistically be able to travel to a child minder or nursery (bearing in mind the rush-hour traffic, if that's when you will be driving).

   ⊙ Ask other parents about how they manage and the pros and cons of the childcare they use.

2. Find out what's available near you:

   ⊙ See who is providing your preferred types of childcare locally. For a list of registered child minders and nurseries, contact your local Children's Information Service – you can get the number by calling Childcare Link on 08000 96 02 96 or see the website at www.childcarelink.gov.uk. You could also ask around among other mums, look into nanny agencies or advertise.

   ⊙ Phone round first to check that there's likely to be a place available for your child at the time you would need it.

   ⊙ Check out two or three examples of the type of childcare you have chosen, so you have something to compare each one against. For a child minder or nursery, visit when there are children there (and perhaps for a second time when there are no children around, when there will be more opportunity to ask questions). See later in the chapter for what to look out for and questions you should ask.

3. Agree the details:

- When you have decided on the person or place you want, sit down together and double-check all the details.

- If you are taking on a child minder or nanny, draw up a contract or agreement covering pay, hours, duties, holidays, sickness and so on.

- If necessary, pay a deposit or retainer fee to secure your child's place.

4. Plan your backup care:

- See if you can think of one or two people, such as a relative or a friend's child minder, who will agree to step in at short notice if your normal childcare arrangement comes unstuck. A child minder may already have someone who does this for her.

5. Settle your child in:

- Introduce him to the child minder or nursery and gradually get him used to staying there, at first with you and then without you (see below).

Carol says:

At three months Christie went into a day nursery, very close to home, which had a baby unit. We knew the lady who owned the nursery, the staff were all qualified in childcare, and I was very comfortable with it.

On the days I wasn't working, I didn't put her in the nursery. I was working about three days a week at that point.

My sister Margaret also helped out if Christie was unwell or whenever my husband and I couldn't manage things between us. Her children had virtually grown up and she was happy to help – it was nice for Christie too.

I don't think anyone feels a hundred per cent guilt-free about it. At first, I tortured myself about leaving Christie. Actually she was quite happy with a cuddle and a bottle from Auntie Margaret or Daddy or whoever – but you feel in your heart 'it's me that she needs!'

I should have enjoyed those early times more, when she was comfortable with anyone.

Here are your main childcare options.

A child minder

A child minder looks after children in her own home. She can mind up to three under-fives at any one time (including her own). She may look after older children after school, too, but no more than six under-eights altogether.

A child minder is likely to develop a warm relationship with your child. Child minders can give individual attention and the opportunity to form a close attachment – both so important to babies.

Most are mums who do it because they want to combine working with looking after their own children. They are likely to do things during the day such as supermarket shopping, visits to friends, maybe a few household chores – the kind of things you would probably be doing with your child if you were at home.

They are self-employed and deal with their own tax and National Insurance payments, so you don't actually employ a child minder – she contracts with you to offer you a service, for which you pay her an hourly rate. She will probably have her own contract that she uses with all parents, which she will ask you to sign.

Child minders must be registered with the education inspectorate, OFSTED. Once a year, an inspector will check out whether the child minder's home is safe and has the right facilities. Criminal record checks are carried out on the child minder and on any other adults in the house. The child minder should have public liability insurance which covers both her and you if your child is involved in an accident or if property is lost or damaged.

Visit several child minders before you make up your mind. Before you make the final decision, you will want to see how she interacts with your child and, if possible, see her with the other children that she will be looking after at the same time.

What to ask

⊙ Ask to see proof of registration and insurance.

⊙ Ask to see her OFSTED report.

⊙ Ask for references from a couple of other parents whose children she looks (or has looked) after.

⊙ Ask what training or experience she has.

⊙ Ask which other children she will be looking after at the same time as yours.

⊙ What is her daily routine and what activities does she provide for the children?

⊙ If your child is a toddler, will he be able to play outside?

⊙ If she will be taking your child anywhere by car, is she insured for minding activities and does she have enough safety restraints for all the children who will be travelling in the car?

⊙ What 'rules' does she have for the children? How does she handle conflict between the children? What does she regard as 'naughty' behaviour, if anything, and how does she handle it?

⊙ Does she provide after-school or holiday care for older children?

⊙ When the time comes, would she be prepared to take your child to playgroup or nursery?

⊙ What sort of meals does she provide?

⊙ What are her views on television, discipline, potty training or anything else that's important to you?

⊙ Does she, or anyone else in the house, smoke? Do they have pets? She should offer to let you see the parts of the house and garden that your child would use.

Questions to ask yourself

⊙ Do you like her?

⊙ Does your child like her?

⊙ Does she share your views on the issues that matter to you? Does she listen to what you want and is she happy to go along with your approach?

⊙ Is there a happy atmosphere in the house?

What the contract should cover

⊙ Her fees.

⊙ A retainer fee or deposit to secure a place.

⊙ Bank Holiday arrangements.

⊙ Annual holidays – yours and hers.

⊙ What happens when your child (or your child minder) is ill.

⊙ Extra hours.

⊙ Playgroup or nursery attendance, if appropriate.

⊙ Reviewing the contract.

- Terminating the contract (how much notice is required on both sides).

- Any other points, such as special dietary needs and who pays for your child's food and nappies.

Advantages

- The security of official vetting.

- Your child is in a friendly 'home from home', probably with other children.

- Babies need to form attachments to a few special people and will be able to do this more easily with a child minder.

- She is likely to be friendly with other minders, which means outings with other children.

- If you're lucky she may even be able to arrange backup care for when she isn't available – for instance, she and another minder could provide cover for each other in the case of illness or holidays.

- She will probably take your child to local activities and playgroup or nursery, when the time comes.

- If you need flexible care because of shift work or working late, a child minder is more likely to be able to provide this than a nursery.

- Child minders offer continuity: you're probably not thinking this far ahead when you go back to work after maternity leave, but eventually, when your child starts school, she may even provide after-school and holiday care.

- If you've just had your first baby you're *definitely* not thinking of this, but when you have your next baby, she will probably be able to look after both children together.

Disadvantages

⊙ If your child is ill or infectious, he won't be able to go to the child minder because of the risk of infecting other children.

⊙ Child minders are only human and they get ill, have family crises and go on holiday like everyone else.

⊙ You may feel that, because your child is in the child minder's home, you have less control over what he eats and who he spends his day with, compared with employing a nanny.

Cost

The cost per week varies a lot depending on where you live, but a survey by the Daycare Trust in 2006 found that the average is around £132 a week for a full-time place. That's over £6,800 a year.

For advice and a copy of its guide to choosing a home childcarer, contact the National Childminding Association (see page 173).

The Families, Children and Childcare Project asked 1,200 mothers when their children were three months old what they thought would be the ideal childcare, money no object. About half the mothers wanted to care for their babies themselves (and went on to do so). Grandparents were top of the list for care provided by someone other than themselves. Only four per cent cited child minders as their ideal.

When questioned again when their children were ten months old, child minding was both the most used and most preferred option. More than half of those using childcare had child minders, and child minding received more top ratings than any other type of childcare.

Your own parents or a friend

Researchers say that in future, grandmothers are more likely to have demanding jobs or careers of their own, to be enjoying high-risk sports or holidaying in exotic places rather than sitting at home waiting to look after your kids. Many grandparents, while they may be happy to spend quality time with the kids, don't want to spend all week looking after them. And, of course, many working couples don't have relatives living close enough to make it an option.

However, informal care by family, friends and neighbours is still actually the most common form of childcare. Although it is not registered and inspected in the way that other types of childcare are, many parents find that it works well for them. And if you have to go back to work but you can't afford to pay for childcare, it can be a lifesaver.

Many parents combine care from a family member with another type of childcare. Close relatives who are caring for your child don't have to register as a child minder.

If one of your friends is going to care for your child in her own home on a regular basis and be paid for it, she will need to register as a child minder (and this can take some time, so plan ahead). She will need to be registered by OFSTED in England (or, if you live in Wales, the Care Standards Inspectorate for Wales). Her home will have to be inspected to make sure it is safe and suitable, she must be insured, have first-aid training, and have a criminal record check carried out – as must anyone else aged over sixteen who lives in her home.

However, if you and a friend are looking after each other's children on a reciprocal basis, provided no money is changing hands, then you don't need to register.

If you are relying on your mum or anyone else who hasn't been trained in childcare, at least make sure this person has some first-aid training so that she would know what to do in an emergency.

Questions to ask yourself

- Does your relative really want to do it or would she be doing it because she feels obliged or doesn't want to let you down?

- Where would she look after your child – in your home or her own? If it's in her house, how suitable and safe is it for a baby or toddler?

- How would your child spend his day? What activities would she do with him?

- Do you and your relative or friend have the same approach to childcare? If not, how happy would she be to do things your way?

- Do you have a good enough relationship to be able to discuss issues without getting personal or fraught?

- Even if she enjoys seeing your child, does she have the patience and the energy to look after a demanding baby or toddler for however long you would need her to do it?

- If a close relative is going to look after your child, paying her for childcare means that you won't end up feeling indebted. If she won't accept any money, is there a risk that she won't take the job seriously enough, or that she will eventually start feeling put upon?

- Will your baby have any contact with other children?

- What would happen if she were ill or unable to look after your child for a few days?

Advantages

- Having a relative look after your baby gives him a secure start in familiar surroundings, and you have the comfort of knowing he is with someone who dotes on him (almost) as much as you do.

- Your baby will get individual attention and be able to form a close attachment to one carer.

⊙ It can also be a lot more affordable, as your mum or mother-in-law is unlikely to demand the going rate! If you work part-time and you have a friend in the same situation, looking after each other's children on the days you don't work could be a good – and free – solution for you both.

⊙ If your friend or relative lives near you, it can be easy to combine this with another type of childcare – for instance if your child goes to nursery in the mornings, grandma could pick him up from there and look after him at home until you get back from work. Or you could have a child minder for three or four days a week, with grandma doing the remaining days.

⊙ You don't have the responsibility of employing someone.

⊙ Your child will grow up with strong family bonds if looked after by a grandparent.

Disadvantages

⊙ Some mothers and mothers-in-law may be less willing than a child minder or nanny to defer to your wishes on issues to do with bringing up your child.

⊙ Your child may spend less time in the company of other children, compared with alternative types of childcare.

⊙ You may feel more comfortable having more of a 'professional' relationship with your child's carer.

⊙ With unregistered childcare like this, at the moment you are not eligible for help towards the costs that you might otherwise be able to claim through the tax credit system.

Cost

You'll need to agree this with your relative, of course, but it's likely to be a lot less than the alternatives.

If you want to pay but they won't accept cash, perhaps you could buy something special for their home every so often or even treat them to a holiday instead.

Sonya Maghie, 33, owns a hairdressing salon. She and her husband have one daughter, Madeline, who is almost a year old. Sonya's friend Elizabeth Bhagat works in the salon and has a daughter the same age, called Tia. Sonya and Elizabeth both work two days a week and swap childcare one day a week.

We both went back to work when the babies were five months old. Liz works on Mondays and Tuesdays, and I work Wednesdays and Thursdays. On one of the days that Liz works I have Tia and on the other, Liz's mum looks after her. On one of the days I work, Liz looks after Madeline for me and on the other, my mother-in-law has her. It works brilliantly!

Liz and I have known each other for years – we trained together and she came to work with me when I bought the salon twelve years ago. We were both trying for a baby at the same time and I had Madeline six weeks before Liz had Tia.

I didn't want to ask my mother-in-law to look after Madeline for more than a day a week because I didn't want it to become a chore for her; I wanted her to enjoy it. My sister was going to look after Madeline on another day but as it got closer, she decided that she would not be able to do it, so I thought I would only be able to work one day a week.

Paying for a child minder would have been difficult for Liz and she said, 'There's no way I want my baby to go to a stranger' – but I wanted her to come back to work. That's when I had the idea that Liz and I could help each other out.

We both feel happy about this because the girls know us. I actually think it's really healthy for the babies to be with other people. Madeline and Tia have a wonderful time!

They were both just starting to get to a clingy stage when we went back to work, but this stopped it.

It is like having twins – they are both crawling now. We bought a double buggy between us so we can take them for walks. At the moment it is hard work but it's lovely to see them together – when Madeline and Tia see each other, they get really excited.

The way we look at it is, we actually work three days. On Fridays, when neither of us is working, we meet up and take the girls swimming. The girls are being brought up together and we are hoping they will grow up to be best friends like us.

I wouldn't want to do it any other way and I would recommend it to anyone else who's in a position to do it.

Day nursery

These provide full daycare, often for babies, toddlers and preschool children (though some do not take under-twos). The hours are geared towards working parents, for instance 8 a.m. to 6 p.m., and they are open all year round.

In areas where demand is high, it may be difficult to find a place, especially for a baby. You may need to put your name on a waiting list and wait for a place to become free.

Whoever runs the nursery – and it may be private or run by the council or even a workplace nursery – it must be registered and inspected by OFSTED (the school and childcare inspection service). There are minimum standards laid down for the premises and the ratio of adults to children: in general, one carer to three children under two; one carer to four children aged two to three; and one carer to eight children aged between three and five. The nursery's OFSTED report will tell you something about the quality of the nursery education and care, as well as the equipment and facilities. You can ask the nursery if you can see a copy of the report or look it up for yourself on the website www.ofsted.gov.uk. But, once you have visited two or three nurseries and asked questions, your own gut feelings are probably just as useful as any report.

Questions to ask yourself

⊙ Would your child enjoy spending a busy day with lots of other children and several adults or would he be happier in a quieter, more homely environment?

⊙ Do the children seem happy and well occupied?

⊙ How responsive are the adults to the children's needs and conversation? Do they listen? Do the adults play with them?

⊙ Is the nursery bright, attractive and clean, and does it have a safe outside play area?

Questions to ask the nursery

⊙ Will your baby get the individual attention and consistent care he needs, from one familiar person? (Babies need to be cared for in a small group with a 'key worker' so they can develop an attachment to the person caring for them.)

⊙ What is the routine of a typical day, and will your child be able to sleep when he needs to?

⊙ What are the nursery policies on issues that are important to you, such as behaviour, discipline and diet?

⊙ How many of the staff have a childcare qualification?

⊙ What is staff turnover like?

Advantages

⊙ It's a safe, stimulating environment that will offer continuity.

⊙ Older children get the chance to make their own friends.

⊙ A nursery is open all year round so you don't have the problem of fitting in with your child minder's or nanny's holidays or finding replacement childcare when she is ill.

Disadvantages

⊙ Places can be hard to come by and expensive in some areas.

⊙ Your child will have to fit in with the nursery regime and the larger group of children.

⊙ He may pick up more coughs, colds and other bugs.

⊙ Even if the nursery is open all year round, you will need some backup care for when your child can't go because he has something infectious.

Cost

According to the Daycare Trust survey, the typical cost of a full-time nursery place for a child under two is £142 a week. That's over £7,300 a year, a rise of 27 per cent in five years. In inner London, the averages go up to £197 a week or over £10,000 a year.

Some employers provide workplace nurseries, charging fees that are subsidised or on a sliding scale depending on the parent's earnings.

For more information on choosing a nursery, contact the National Day Nurseries Association (details on page 174).

Nursery classes and playgroups

Most nursery classes and nursery schools, intended as preparation for school, open only in school hours and term-times. Some are attached to primary schools, while others are private or run by the local authority.

Playgroups are run by trained early-years professionals, but parents are heavily involved too. Most offer sessional care, i.e.

mornings *or* afternoons, but some can provide extended day care that may meet the needs of some working parents.

Unless you are working part-time, you will need to combine this option with another type of childcare, such as a relative or child minder who will drop your child off in the morning and pick him up later in the day. You may also have to sort out childcare for the holidays. Four-year-olds and some three-year-olds are entitled to five free sessions a week in a registered early education setting.

Questions to ask

⊙ How many of the staff and helpers are qualified in childcare?

⊙ What activities are on offer?

⊙ What is the structure of each session?

⊙ How well do the adults relate to the children?

⊙ How much choice will your child have in what he does while he's there?

⊙ How will the staff share information with you about your child?

⊙ Nurseries and playgroups are inspected by OFSTED, so ask if you can have a look at the report.

Advantages

⊙ They are usually relatively affordable.

⊙ The social and educational activities are a good preparation for school.

⊙ They're good if you work from home.

⊙ Your child may make friends who will eventually go to the same school.

Disadvantages

⊙ Unless it fits in with your working hours, you have to dovetail it with another type of care.

⊙ If your child isn't yet toilet-trained, they might not accept him.

⊙ Your child will have to fit in with the structure of the nursery or pre-school and with a large group of children.

Cost

If the nursery school is part of the state education system it is usually free. Pre-schools and playgroups charge on a sessional basis, usually £3 to £5 per session. Private nursery schools are likely to charge more.

Government grant funding

Free part-time places in early education (in some kind of registered pre-school group setting) are available for all three and four year olds before they start school.

The funding does not go to the parents – the nursery or pre-school claims it from the government. But as it is for a limited number of hours, you may still need to find and pay for 'top-up' care.

Your early education provider or local Children's Information Service will be able to give you more information about this.

Carol says:

Jodie has just started nursery school now, in the mornings. Being the third child, she is ready for it much earlier than the other two would have been – she's desperate to get there and goes running in! She has her own friends now, just like Robbie and Christie.

A nanny

A nanny is someone who ideally has both qualifications in child-care and some previous experience, who will come to your house each day or live in. Either way, it spares you the hassle of getting your child breakfasted, dressed and out of the house each morning when you leave for work.

Having a nanny makes life a lot easier in some ways, but it's not a cheap option. If you have two children (or more!), however, it becomes less expensive in comparison to other types of child-care, where you have to pay twice over if you have two children.

Most nannies like to negotiate their salaries in net terms, leaving the payment of income tax and National Insurance to their employers. So when doing your sums, add on the nanny's income tax and both her and your (employer's) National Insurance contributions on top of her take-home pay. You can't get out of this – paying your nanny cash in hand could land you with a jail sentence and a fine of up to £5,000!

However, you could bring the cost down considerably if you were to share your nanny with another family. You could ask around among your friends or advertise locally to find other parents in the same situation who might want to come in with you. You'd have to decide whose house the nanny was going to be based in, how the cost would be shared if you don't both work the same hours and sort out lots of other issues, like whether you share a similar approach to bringing up children.

You could find a nanny through a nanny agency (allow for the agency fees when you are doing your sums), which you can find listed in Yellow Pages, or you could advertise via your local paper, specialist magazines such as *Nursery World*, or through your local Jobcentre.

The Professional Association of Nursery Nurses believes a nanny should have at least two years' childcare experience before having sole charge of a young baby. But if your child is older and you don't mind taking on someone newly qualified, you could contact local colleges to let them know that you will have a vacancy for someone completing a childcare course.

Nannies don't have to be officially vetted or registered unless they work for three families or more.

For an information pack on employing a nanny, contact the Professional Association of Nursery Nurses (details on page 176).

Whichever route you choose to find your nanny, make sure you allow yourself plenty of time before you have to go back to work. That way you won't be forced to settle for a nanny you are not completely sure about. Always check references and qualifications carefully – don't rely on a nanny agency to do this.

Checking out prospective nannies

⊙ Interview the nanny yourself.

⊙ Ask for references from previous employers and don't rely on written references – phone them up. If a referee doesn't seem to be saying much, ask the killer question: 'Would you employ this nanny again?' If she says no, alarm bells should ring loud and clear.

⊙ Ask to see originals of the nanny's childcare qualifications. If in doubt, make a note of the awarding body and the reference number so that, later on, you can contact the awarding body to confirm that the nanny has the qualification.

⊙ Ask to see a passport (the original not a photocopy) so you can be sure the nanny has given you her correct name.

⊙ As a private individual, you are not eligible to carry out a Criminal Records Bureau check to see whether the nanny has anything in her past that would make her an unsuitable candidate to work with children. But a nanny agency may have these checks done.

SureStart, the government programme, covers early education, childcare, health and family support. See the website at www. surestart.gov.uk.

Questions to ask yourself

⊙ How do you feel about someone being in your home all day with your child?

⊙ How do you feel about being an employer, with all that this involves?

⊙ Will your nanny know other nannies or go to mother and toddler clubs so that your child will be able to mix with other children?

⊙ If you are taking on a live-in nanny, will she be 'one of the family' outside working hours?

⊙ Would you be prepared to share your nanny with another family?

⊙ Do her views on bringing up children give you confidence that you share the same approach?

⊙ What house rules will you lay down for the nanny? Would you let her invite friends into your home? What about smoking in her room? According to the Professional Association of Nursery Nurses it is issues like this, rather than the way the nanny looks after the child, that often cause problems. It's essential to sit down together at the beginning and discuss your expectations, so that you both know where you stand.

Advantages

⊙ It can be a cost-effective option if you have more than one child.

⊙ A nanny may be the best way to manage childcare if you work unusual hours or shifts.

⊙ You can bring down the cost by finding another family for a nanny-share.

⊙ You and your child can build a strong personal relationship with the nanny.

⊙ Your child gets lots of individual attention.

⊙ You have quite a lot of say in what the nanny does with your child, what she gives him to eat and so on.

⊙ Your child is based in his own home (or perhaps his own plus one other, if you are sharing).

⊙ Your nanny may agree to do a few chores, such as washing children's clothes or making tea; you could even negotiate some babysitting as well, if you have a live-in nanny.

⊙ If your child is slightly poorly, but not so bad that you have to stay off work, he can stay at home with the nanny. A child minder or nursery might be reluctant to take him.

Disadvantages

⊙ If you have only one child, having a nanny is usually one of the more expensive options – and there are also hidden costs such as heating the house all day.

⊙ A nanny is not a 'registered' form of childcare – which means you cannot claim tax credits towards the cost of paying her salary, in the way that you might (if eligible) claim towards nursery or child-minder fees.

⊙ Being an employer means extra paperwork for you. You will have to set up an employment contract as well as keeping on top of the tax and National Insurance payments.

⊙ Unless she knows other nannies, there's a risk that she could be rather isolated – especially if she is uncomfortable taking your child to places where the other women are mostly mums.

⊙ You (or your partner) may feel you lose some of your privacy, especially if you have a live-in nanny.

⊙ Nanny-sharing takes a lot of organisation – imagine trying to plan holiday dates that suit two families as well as the nanny.

Cost

Employing a nanny can cost from £250 to £400 a week, plus tax and National Insurance.

Carol says:

When Christie was nearly four, her nursery changed hands and I was not happy with the new owners. I felt that it didn't have the personal touch any more, I thought the girls were too young and inexperienced and I wasn't sure all the time who was looking after her.

So I approached one of the nursery nurses who had looked after Christie since the beginning about becoming a nanny for us.

We were unbelievably lucky with Wendy. She was uncomfortable with the new owners as well and was thinking of leaving, so the timing all worked out. She has known every one of our children since birth and I feel that's really nice.

She lived about five miles away and worked from Monday to Friday, eight in the morning till six in the evening. At other times Alex and I could do quite a lot of the childcare between the two of us but if a situation arose where we couldn't, my sister Margaret would always help.

Wendy was great because she did lots of home cooking and the children got lots of fresh air and did the things that we would do with them if we were there.

I am completely comfortable with the two key people who

helped us with the childcare, Wendy and Margaret. The chemistry worked – Wendy knew when to make herself scarce and she knew when we really needed her.

If you make a decision to work, for whatever reason, you can't possibly go to work unless you are absolutely sure the children are happy with the arrangement. I dread to think what would have happened if we'd lost our nanny. I would hate to have had to start all over again – I would have really worried about having a stranger come in.

An au pair

Au pairs come to the UK to learn English while working for and living with a family. However, they are unlikely to have any child-care qualifications or experience, their English may not be very good and they are likely to stay for only six months to a year – so an au pair is not going to be the answer to your childcare prayers. However, it could work if you have older children who simply need to be met from school and looked after for an hour or so until you get home.

You'll need to arrange English classes for your au pair and help her to meet friends of her own age. You can find an au pair through an agency.

Help from the taxman

As well as Child Tax Credit, you may be able to claim Working Tax Credit if you and your partner (or you, if you are a lone parent) are working, whether employed or self-employed, on low or middle incomes. This tax credit has a 'childcare element' that is paid to help working parents who have to spend money on childcare.

The amount you get depends on your income, the number of hours you work, the number and age of your children and the amount you pay for childcare.

You must work at least 16 hours a week. You can apply while you are on maternity leave – but if it's your first baby, you have to wait until the baby is born before you apply.

The scheme is administered through the Inland Revenue and is normally paid through the pay packet to people who are employees.

To find out more, phone the information helpline on 0845 300 3900 or visit the website www.taxcredits.inlandrevenue.gov.uk.

School-aged children

Many child minders are happy to meet children from a nearby school and look after them until parents get home from work. Just as if you were looking for full-time care, try to look at the carer, her home and the set-up through your child's eyes. Will he be able to do what he wants to do when he gets in after school, whether that's starting his homework or simply relaxing in front of the television? Will there be other children of his age or will they all be babies and toddlers?

Your local Childcare Information Service will tell you if there are any breakfast clubs or after-school clubs near you. These are based at schools or in community centres and the like, and there may be staff who can collect your child from school and take him to the club. If you are lucky enough to have access to a club like this it can be a good option, as it's convenient and your child will be with other children of the same age. Again, it's important that he can choose what to do and that there's a place to sit and be quiet as well as join in with games and lively activities.

School holiday care is the most difficult type of care to find, so start planning in good time. As well as taking some of your own annual leave, you may need to mix and match a combination of solutions to meet your school holiday childcare needs:

⊙ Some after-school clubs also run play schemes during the school holidays.

⊙ Alternatively, some local authorities and private organisations offer holiday courses in sports and other interests, led by experienced play leaders. These are fun for your child but, because of the hours they are open, rarely solve all your childcare problems if you work full-time. You might be able to arrange for someone else to take your child there and meet him when it finishes, or perhaps arrange to work a shorter day during this period so that you can do this yourself.

⊙ A number of private companies run American-style summer camps and day camps for unaccompanied children during the school holidays, with a wide variety of multi-activity and specialist courses on offer. Check out the centre carefully and think about whether this is something your child would enjoy.

⊙ Many parents cope with holidays by calling on relatives and friends, especially friends with children of the same age. Even if your parents don't live near enough to offer regular childcare, it could be a treat for both them and your child if he goes to stay for a few days during the school holidays.

⊙ Think laterally – perhaps you could find a child minder who would be able to take your child during the school holidays, if she normally looks after teachers' children in term-time only.

⊙ You could take on a mother's help, such as a university student home for the summer. You still need to draw up an agreement that states clearly what you both expect from the arrangement, even if it is only for a few weeks – this helps prevent misunderstandings and problems.

Going back part-time?

While some child minders won't want to take on children part-time (because this uses up a place which could otherwise have been full-time), others are happy to take on a child on this basis. Nurseries, too, may take two part-timers to fill a full-time place.

If you are planning to use informal childcare, for instance from your mum, the fact that it is for less than a full week may make this more achievable.

Part-time childcare could be more difficult to arrange if you are planning to take on a nanny, though you may be able to find another family looking for part-time childcare and employ the nanny between you on a full-time basis.

Sarah Irons, 36, is a vet in Dorchester, Dorset. She and her husband, who is also a vet, have two children, six-year-old Joseph and Hannah, who is three.

I always wanted to work part-time after taking a reasonable amount of maternity leave. I was aware that there would be a problem with confidence the longer I left it, so I was keen not to lose touch.

When Joseph was born, my husband and I were living in Kenya where he had a job and I did some informal, part-time work as a vet. We came back to the UK when Joseph was eighteen months old. My husband said, 'You find a job first and I will fit around you,' because I had put my career on the back burner for so long and I had been giving him hell!

I was looking for any job I could find and would have taken full-time work if that was all there was, but it just happened that I found the perfect part-time job.

This enabled my husband to take up a PhD post nearby. My job was in Somerset where I worked with a husband-and-wife team who had young children and job-shared between themselves. They were very much into the idea that no one should have to work full-time if they have young kids. It was ideal because they shared the same mentality about work that I had at that stage.

I worked there for two years and then I had Hannah. Six months later I went back to the job, but on a slightly better deal as I didn't have to do any on-call or out-of-hours work. Vets often get called out in the middle of the night!

When my husband finished his PhD he found a job in Dorset, so we moved down here when Hannah was two-and-a-half.

At first I worked as a locum vet in the summer, filling in at different veterinary practices, and one of the practices I worked for offered me a part-time job.

I now do two nine-hour days each week. The question of working evenings and weekends and being on-call was something we had to negotiate. I said I was prepared to do it if it was required but I would accept a lower salary if I did not have to do it. It's not an easy thing to go for, but fortunately the practice was able to accommodate me. The other vets in the practice work one weekend in four but I only do weekends very occasionally, if someone else can't make it.

On the days I work, Hannah goes to a preschool all day and Joe is at school so he goes to an after-school club until my husband can pick him up. There is some childcare out there and it's okay if you are working nine to five, but if you are doing anything else it's a bit difficult. I wouldn't be able to pick up Joe and Hannah until at least six-thirty and the preschool ends at five-thirty, so if my husband is not around I have to ask friends to help me out.

My advice to other mums going back to work is to get your partner in line, if you have one, from the very start! Decide who is taking the kids, who's making the supper, who is doing the lunchboxes. If you are on your own you must have to be terribly organised.

With us, things have just evolved rather than us sitting down at the start and working out the most efficient way of doing it. In my experience, after extreme stress trying to get two *children out of the door, you begin to realise it's not possible and you have to say to your partner, 'You're going to have to do this.' It has been a painful process for us in some respects – it's probably different for different people.*

The other problem is that we have moved around a lot. But now that we have been here a year, I have various friends nearby who can help me out if my arrangements go pear-shaped. My neighbour and I help each other out by dropping off at school or picking up and it works well. When you move around a lot or you live in a big city where you don't know anyone, it's more difficult. Often there is just half an hour when you can't be somewhere, and if you have someone who can hang on to the kids for that time, it's such a benefit.

My ideal job would be five mornings a week – but of course no other vet in a practice wants to work just afternoons and evenings! For me, two days a week is a good amount to feel you are using your skills and keeping up to date, but you have enough time at home to do the weekly shop and keep up with housework without having to employ a cleaner. If I worked a four or five-day week everything else would slip.

But when both children are at school I think I would be a bit bored with a two-day week and will probably want to do more.

Settling him in

Introduce your child to the new carer or the new nursery and, as the time for your return to work approaches, have a few short trial runs. Stay with him on the first couple of occasions and then leave him for longer and longer periods as he becomes more familiar with the carer.

Don't panic if the first week or so is tricky – chances are he will soon settle down (and so will you!).

When he doesn't want you to go

Some babies and children will wave you off to work happily, but sometimes there are hiccups. There's nothing harder than leaving a sobbing child who's clinging on to you for dear life. Try not to have long, lingering farewells but on the other hand, don't sneak out without saying goodbye either.

If it's hard leaving a baby, it can be even worse with an older child who can tell you that he doesn't want to go to the nursery or even beg you not to go to work. Your child will pick up on your own mood – if you are anxious or upset, it won't help, so try to be brave while he can still see you, even if you break down in a sobbing heap when you get to your car.

Children usually settle quickly once their parents are out of sight, so don't go on feeling anxious or upset about it all day. If it helps, phone the child minder or nursery once you get to work. With luck, they will be able to reassure you that he stopped crying within a few minutes and is now playing happily.

Carol says:

If I'm honest, there are times when my children don't want me to go to work. It is usually when they are tired. But at that point you are committed and you just have to go. And when you come back, they are absolutely fine – they have forgotten about the time you went away, because now something else is happening.

Getting on with your child's carer

Whoever cares for your child while you're at work – whether it's your mum, sister, a child minder, a nanny or nursery staff – you'll want to have a good working relationship with them.

Regular communication is vital

If there's no time to have a chat at the beginning or end of each day, try to arrange a time at least once a week when you can talk without interruptions. You might manage this by arriving earlier than usual on one day a week, or even scheduling a regular weekly telephone call in the evening. Even if there's nothing that you want to ask her, there may be things that she would like to ask you or tell you about your child or the arrangements.

Choose your moment

If there's something you'd like her to do that she's not doing – or something she is doing that you'd rather she didn't – the best approach is to say it openly rather than dropping hints, which can easily be missed or misinterpreted. Tact and diplomacy are obviously vital here. Your tone needs to be warm and friendly – so choose a time when you are feeling fairly relaxed and positive rather than blurting it out when you are in a foul mood or rushing off to work.

Be punctual

We all have travel crises and other emergencies from time to time that delay us, but if it happens regularly, your minder will start to feel that you are taking advantage or that you think her time doesn't matter. So it's only fair to make every effort to bring and collect your child on time – not to mention paying fees on time.

Let her know how much you appreciate her

Christmas and birthday presents are always welcome, of course, but a simple and heartfelt 'Thank you – I don't know what I'd do without you' means a lot too.

Keep your own rules

Suppose your mum or a nanny looks after your child in your home and you have asked her not to allow him biscuits before tea or to let him spread out his railway set in the middle of the living-room floor. It's probably fair to say that she won't be too impressed if you allow him to do these things when you are at home – and your child will get confused too.

Carol says:

The kids try it on sometimes: they'd come to me and say, 'Can I have a biscuit?' and I'd say, 'Did you ask Wendy?'

'Yes.'

'And what did she say?'

'No.'

So while Wendy was in the house and she said something goes, then I never overruled her. The children really respected her, they didn't run all over her – in fact, at times I think they were better behaved for her than they are for me, which is a bit frustrating!

Jealousy

Some mums' greatest fear is that their baby will come to prefer the nanny or child minder to them. Unless you are working such long hours that your child really does hardly ever see you, there is no risk of him forgetting who mummy is.

The nature and strength of a baby's attachments depend on the adults' emotional involvement and responsiveness to him. Babies need to develop a close attachment with at least one person in the first year as a basis for healthy psychological development. But they are capable of forming attachments to several adults – so forming a bond with a child minder or nanny doesn't mean that he will love you any less. It is a positive thing for your child to have a good relationship with his carer. With a small number of consistent carers, babies learn that relationships are a source of comfort, reassurance and love.

Sometimes children do react by bursting into tears when you pick them up at the end of the day or having a terrible tantrum the minute they get home. If this happens, see it as your child's way of releasing his feelings at the end of a long day. He feels he can 'let go' now that he is back with you. It's hard for you, of course, but it doesn't mean he doesn't love you or that he would rather stay with the child minder than go home.

For more information on childcare options and how to pay for childcare, contact the Daycare Trust (see page 170) or get a free copy of *Looking for Childcare? A Sure Start guide to help you make the right choice* from the Department for Education and Skills on 0845 602 2260 or dfes@prolog.uk.com.

Chapter 5:
Sleep, and how to have more of it

There can't be many working mothers – come to that, there probably aren't many mothers – who are happy with the amount of sleep they get.

When you first have a baby, the reality of having to wake for night feeds can come as a hideous shock. It's not only parents with young babies who have to contend with lack of sleep, though – some babies continue to wake up at night for the whole of the first year. And while broken nights are awful, so is rising at the crack of dawn with a baby or toddler who thinks five o'clock is a good time to start the day.

While you are on maternity leave after having your first baby, you might get the chance to have a lie-in in the morning or catch up on your sleep with the odd daytime nap here and there while your baby is asleep. But of course, once you are back at work you somehow have to get through the working day while suffering from sleep deprivation – sometimes for weeks or months on end.

You know the feeling: the alarm clock goes off in the morning, you reach over groggily to switch it off and would kill for another hour in bed. All day long you feel irritable with everyone, you're too lethargic to do anything, you have difficulty concentrating, there are times when you can barely stay awake, and it feels as though you'll never be normal again.

> *Carol says:*
>
> Sleep deprivation is probably the worst form of torture I have ever experienced.

After my first child the thought of getting up in the night, probably more than anything else, almost put me off the idea of having any more. You have the elation of having the baby but at the back of your mind you know that you are not going to sleep now for at least three months.

I have found that my friends have all been through that same desolate feeling in the middle of the night, when you feel as though you are the only person in the world who is watching rubbish on television to try to stay awake to get a few ounces of milk into a baby. Then at the end of it, the child pukes and brings the whole lot back up and you just want to weep – it's horrible!

I was bottle-feeding and every ounce of milk I could get into Christie gave me another hour of sleep. If I could get her to have three ounces I would get three hours of sleep. And often I would have to be up the next morning for work. Eventually I said to Alex: 'You have to do this some nights, because I just can't do it every night.'

When your child won't sleep

If your child hates the thought of going to bed in the evening or is waking up crying in the night, here are a few tips.

⊙ Have a regular, calm and enjoyable evening routine so your baby knows that bedtime is on the way. For instance a bath, a bottle or breast-feed and a cuddle, a song, a bedtime story and a goodnight kiss.

⊙ Make night-time as different as possible from daytime so that he can learn the difference – for instance, don't bring him downstairs again once he's been put to bed in the evening.

⊙ Try leaving your toddler or older child in bed listening to music or a story from a cassette or CD, with the lights out. Chances are he will drop off before it finishes.

The aim is to get your child into his cot and let him drop off by himself, but unfortunately some babies will have no truck with this. They protest loud and long if you stop holding and rocking them or – horror of horrors! – dare to try and leave the room before they are asleep.

Some babies do seem to need to cry for a few minutes before they go off to sleep. Others just won't settle at all. But if you don't want to go through the trauma of training your child to go to sleep without you in the evenings, perhaps it could prove easier to train yourself to see the 'problem' in a different light. As you sit there stroking his back or rocking him to get him to drop off, try not to spend that time stressing about how much you have to fit in when you finally get downstairs for the evening. Persuade yourself that this time is an opportunity to unwind and relax after a long day, a quiet time to enjoy being with your child.

Older children can be just as insistent – many a working mum is so exhausted by the evening that she lies down on her child's bed to try to get him to go to sleep, and drops off before he does. We've all done this, and woken up two hours later feeling worse than before.

What if an older baby, past the night-feeds stage, regularly cries at night and this continues for weeks or months?

Some experts advocate the 'controlled crying' approach. This means you don't pick up your child or 'reward' him in any way for crying. Instead, you simply go in to reassure him every five minutes or so, talk to him and perhaps pat his back, then leave the room – even if he continues to protest. The idea is that after a few nights of this, he will learn that crying won't work, accept the fact that he has to go to sleep without you there, and start sleeping through. But some people feel that you should not leave a baby to cry under any circumstances, and that a crying baby should be comforted.

This is a tricky one for any parent, but it's even worse if you're a working mum. If we can't be there for our child during the day, then when they cry for us at night we feel we haven't got a leg to stand on. If you could never contemplate leaving your child to cry, you're not alone.

If you have a partner, share the night shift. Take it in turns to get up, or split the night into two so that both of you can have a good few uninterrupted hours. (If your partner suffers from selective deafness, as many do, a dig in the ribs may be called for.)

There are loads of different approaches to solving sleep problems – you need to find one that you are happy with and that works for you. The best thing to do is to read up on the subject in baby books and magazines, or talk to your health visitor and your friends, and decide on an approach that you and your partner feel comfortable with. What works for one baby may not work for another. There's no right or wrong but, whatever you choose, try to be consistent and give it a chance to work.

And remember, however hard this period is, it won't last for ever.

Carol says:

Christie kept waking for the first few months, which was about right – then after that, she was just trying it on and I was too guilt-ridden to see it. As soon as I walked into the room, she would stop crying. It wasn't because she wanted milk – she wanted to sit up and play and chat.

Of course it wasn't anything to do with me going out to work, but I would torture myself that it was. It's just what children do, whether you are there all day or not.

Alex and I would lie awake, arguing with each other.

'It's because of me.'

'Don't be so stupid, woman, it's not because of you!'

'It is, it's my fault.'

'Oh, for goodness' sake, if we don't stop this now, we'll be up all night for the rest of our lives.'

We read the books and listened to what everyone else said about it. Eventually Alex said: 'Next time you go away on one of your trips, I'll sort this out' – and he did.

I was away for three nights. He said the first night she cried for three hours, the second for two hours, then an hour-and-a-half. The next night it was an hour. It was terrible. I couldn't have done it myself – but one of you has to be strong enough to do it.

I can laugh about it now but at the time it was quite stressful. It gets much easier with the second and third children. They are never so demanding because you don't have the time to give to them that you had with the first.

Make his daytime naps work for you

You want to see your child after work, of course, but you also need a little time to yourself after he's gone to bed. But what if he won't go until nine or ten in the evening? Perhaps your child simply isn't ready for bed before then because of his daytime routine.

Babies up to twelve months usually still need two naps a day, but by eighteen months or so, one might be enough. If he's had a long, late afternoon nap at the nursery or the child minder's, he may simply not be tired enough to want to sleep again at seven or eight in the evening. You and your child's carer know him best, so try to work something out between you. You can't expect her to keep a tired child going for hours – babies and toddlers need to sleep during the day to recharge their batteries. But perhaps she could gradually move his nap to an earlier time of day, drop one of the naps or gently wake him up a bit sooner.

When your toddler first drops his second daytime nap, he may start to get fretful by late afternoon or early evening. But this tricky period will pass as he gets used to less sleep. A bath can help to soothe an overtired, ratty toddler.

Perhaps you have the opposite problem – you've been at work all day and want your baby to go to bed later so you can spend some time with him when you come home. To make sure that your child still gets enough sleep, talk to his minder about gradually changing his daytime nap in the other direction. If it's possible for her to get your baby to have his nap later in the day, or to leave him to sleep for longer, he should be able to stay awake until a bit later in the evening.

Carol says:

When my kids were babies and they were starting to drop off to sleep at the wrong time, I used to wipe their faces with a damp flannel to try and say: 'No, you're not going to do this – there's a couple more hours to go.'

It sounds heartless, doesn't it! But for me, the sooner they are into a routine of 'this is when you sleep, this is when you eat', the better.

Getting through the working day

Most working mums probably have to manage on less sleep than they would ideally like, at least for a while. There are no easy answers, but here are some survival tactics for when you are desperately tired at work and you have to soldier on.

⊙ Does your workplace have a rest room where you could shut your eyes for half an hour in your lunch break? Failing that, is there anywhere else you could go – like your car, for instance? (Take an alarm clock or set the alarm on your mobile phone to make sure you really do go back to work in the afternoon!)

⊙ Falling asleep at your desk? Get up and move around or do some stretching exercises to chase away the tiredness. Drink some coffee or, if you don't like coffee, some cold water.

⊙ If you're in for a long meeting in a stuffy room and you think there's a real danger you could drop off in the middle of it, have a cup of strong coffee beforehand. Open the windows to let some cool reviving air in.

⊙ Splash your face with cold water.

⊙ If you have a friend at work, suggest swapping hand and shoulder massages in your break or lunch hour.

⊙ If you can, schedule your most demanding work tasks at the time of day when you're most alert, and save the routine, boring tasks for the mid-afternoon energy dip.

⊙ When fatigue is a serious problem, accept that in order to catch up on your sleep, some days you may need to go to bed at the same time as your child – even if it's ridiculously early.

Can't get to sleep?

Worrying about work, health or family problems – or sometimes even anticipating the baby waking up – keeps some parents awake at night, so they find that they are tossing and turning even when their child is sleeping well.

Try to relax by visualising yourself in the middle of a peaceful scene such as a woodland waterfall, a beautiful meadow or a sandy beach.

Avoid drinking coffee or eating heavy meals in the evenings, as these can keep you awake (though some people find a milky drink before bed works wonders). Taking some exercise is a good idea, if you can fit it in in the early evening – as long as it's not just before bed.

Perhaps you can't sleep because you are working until late in the evening or you still have work on your mind. Recognise that time to relax is important too – having a night out, watching a funny movie or phoning an old friend to catch up on news will take your mind off work, and you might find you have a better night's sleep for it.

We may think that tiredness is the result of stress, packing so much into the day and rushing around too much. But sometimes you can be incredibly busy and yet still feel full of energy.

The feeling of tiredness sometimes results from a feeling of lack of control over your life. If you are in this situation, accept that you can't do everything all at once – tackle problems one at a time, in small steps (see 'To Do lists', chapter 6) to regain a feeling that you can get on top of things again.

Carol says:

People say that when you have your first baby, you should sleep when the baby sleeps. But you feel you can't because the place is a mess and you end up running round with the vacuum cleaner – it's a stupid thing to do and you shouldn't, but I did!

Allow enough time

You may have a lot to pack in to your day and want to make every minute count, but are you your own worst enemy? Do you find you are constantly rushing from one place to another while worrying about being late? If you are in the habit of cutting it too fine, and then you have an unexpected phone call or get stuck in traffic, the stress and anxiety about getting to your next appointment will add to your fatigue.

So when you are scheduling activities for yourself or your child – whether it's getting to a meeting at another office or picking your child up from the nursery or child minder after work – get in the habit of allowing plenty of time.

And at home, think how much more relaxed you feel on

those mornings when you get up ten minutes earlier than usual. For once, you don't have to charge round the house, grabbing anything you can find in the back of the fridge to stuff in the kids' lunchboxes or emptying the contents of entire cupboards onto the floor as you hunt for missing shoes or school library books.

When you think of how much we working mums manage to achieve in a day, it's no wonder many of us feel tired a lot of the time – anyone would. There's no end to the demands our families – and sometimes our jobs – make on us. Struggling on is all very well, but if you drive yourself beyond a certain point, eventually you may find that your health starts to suffer.

At times like this, a bit of relaxation must be a priority. You owe it to yourself to spend some of your precious time on yourself occasionally, so that you can fit in a few of the things that will help you cope and make you feel better. See The Working Mum's Survival Plan in Chapter 13.

Chapter 6:
Managing your time

Probably the one thing most working women would love above all else would be to have a 'wife' at home. How much easier life would be if there was someone at home all day to look after the house and kids, do the shopping, cooking, washing, ironing and cleaning, make the dentist's appointments and wait in for the gas man.

But short of employing an army of helpers or persuading our partner to become a househusband, it's a question of maximising the time we have got, whether at work or at home, and getting as much done in as short a time as possible.

Time management at home

Many working mums are already expert in time management – we have to be! But here are some ideas and suggestions that might just help you get more organised and manage your precious time a bit better:

Deal with mail straightaway

When you're busy, it's all too easy to end up with piles of paper littering every available surface in your home. Experts advise trying to ensure that each piece of paper passes through your hands only once. In other words, if an item of mail comes through the door, try to process it straight away. Either bin it if it is of no interest, file it if it's something you need to keep for later, or deal with it straight away – for instance, answer it if it's a query or pay it if it's a bill. Keep your recycling bin or basket right next to the front door so that junk mail can go straight into it without even a chance of cluttering up your home.

File paperwork properly

Most of us keep some kind of file of important documents such as birth certificates, passports, mortgage agreements, bank and building society accounts and so on. It's a good idea to keep a separate concertina file with separate sections for all the letters, forms and leaflets relating to 'family' stuff. For instance you may have letters from your child's preschool or school, details of term dates and fees for any clubs or lessons your children attend, contact numbers for your dentist and doctor, the vet and the cattery, the garage where you take the car for servicing and so on. If you tend to be disorganised and leave stuff like this lying around the house in lots of different places so that you can never find it when you need it, you'll find a logical filing system saves you a lot of time.

Don't lose those guarantees

When you buy a new appliance for the house, keep any instruction booklets, guarantees and servicing information together in your 'family file' for future reference. One day it could save you several hours of turning out the contents of all your drawers and cupboards while growling, 'I know I put it somewhere.'

Use a notice board or calendar

Children's parties, football club, ballet classes, dentist's appointments ... noting everything down on a family calendar or notice board is a good idea. It means that both you and your partner can see at a glance what is going on and where all the other members of the family are supposed to be. In lots of families, mum is the one who keeps track of the children's activities and makes a note of them in her diary – which means dad may start to feel it's nothing to do with him, and she feels overwhelmed by having to remember everything. Noting family events on a calendar on the wall makes it more of a shared thing. If you have a partner and he's around, get him to do his share of getting the kids to the right place at the right time.

Prepare the night before

It's easier said than done, but if you can summon up the energy in the evening to get everything you need ready for work the next day, you'll be glad you did. As your child gets older and starts school, encourage him each evening to lay out his clothes and pack his bag with everything he needs for the next day, such as gym or music equipment. Write any notes he needs for school. If he takes a packed lunch, you could even make the sandwiches and keep them in the fridge overnight. It makes the mornings that bit less stressful and saves last-minute panics.

Use direct debits

Arranging to pay as many as possible of your bills by direct debit can save you a lot of time – and it also means there's no risk of forgetting to pay. Remember, some companies give you a discount for paying by direct debit, too.

Shop from home

If schlepping round the shops in the run-up to Christmas, looking for presents, is not your idea of a good time, plan ahead and avoid the crowds – do your Christmas shopping in the comfort of your own home via mail order catalogues or the Internet.

Build up a stock of handy gifts

If you have older children you will probably find that several times a year you have to make an unscheduled trip to the shops to find a last-minute present for them to take to friend's birthday party. Make life easier on yourself by buying nice gifts as and when you see them – next time you need a child's birthday present in a hurry, all you have to do is look through the ones you have stashed away in a drawer.

Plan ahead

At Christmas, as soon as you get your diary or calendar for the coming year, sit down and write in any birthdays you don't want to miss. Start thinking about possible holiday dates too, before anyone else at work bags the time you want.

Time management at work

You might be in a job where your hours are fixed and you can drop everything and leave at 5 p.m. Or you might quite often find it difficult to leave on time because of the workload. Either way, being a working mum concentrates your mind wonderfully. When you have a baby or children at home, you want to get your work done and get out of there!

In some workplaces, it's surprising how much time people spend on things other than actually getting the job done. When you become a working mother you may find that you become much less inclined to spend unproductive time at work, whether it's sitting through a long, unnecessary meeting or standing around the water cooler talking about last night's soaps.

We could all do with a bit more organisation in our lives to help us manage our time more efficiently. With the incentive of getting home on time, why not try a few of these strategies, if you haven't already?

Make 'To do' lists

Too many demands on your time can be stressful. You can also find yourself forgetting to do certain things, putting off tasks that you don't like doing, and spending too much time on trivial tasks. Time management experts swear by 'To do' lists, lists of all the tasks you have to do, placed in order of importance.

Making and maintaining a prioritised list is a simple but powerful way of organising yourself and reducing stress, whether it's to do with your home or your work tasks and commitments. There are various ways of doing this.

One way is the 'ABC' method. In the A section, list all the things that absolutely have to be done that day. In the B section, list the things you have to do that week. In the C section, put tasks that need to be done within a month or so. As the B and C items become more pressing or their deadline approaches, you can move them up to the A or B list. That way you only concern yourself with these tasks when you really need to, and you don't waste time worrying about low priority jobs.

If the tasks still seem overwhelming, break each one down into smaller components and give each of these a priority listing.

Making a list like this provides you with a precise plan that allows you to tackle the tasks facing you in order of their importance, and separates those that really matter from the low-priority ones that eat up your time.

Learn to say 'no'

When someone wants you to take on an extra project, work late or stand in for someone else, it can be hard to refuse. Don't just automatically say, 'Yes, of course,' and then end up regretting it and resenting the time it takes up. Don't be afraid to say, 'I'll have a think about it and get back to you,' so that you have time to decide whether you really do want to take it on or not.

If your time is precious and you already have too much to cope with, you have to be assertive enough to put your own needs (and those of your family) first. Dealing with the conflicting demands of work and family is one of the hardest things about being a working parent, and it's something each of us has to work out through experience.

Deal with the paper mountain

If you work in an office you're likely to find that, just like at home, piles of paper seem to sprout up alarmingly quickly. Again, try to train yourself to deal with each piece of paper as few times as possible. If you just look at it then put it back on the pile, it will end up going through your hands many more times in the next few days or weeks as you search through the pile for something else that you've lost.

So, once again – when a piece of paper comes across your desk, bin it, file it, pass it on or deal with it straight away. Have a good filing system – and use it! – to cut down on time spent looking for lost items.

Don't get distracted by office politics

Getting involved in office politics can be very time-consuming. So don't waste your precious time talking about who's in and who's out, who's on their way up and whose career is going down the pan. In some workplaces, people also spend a lot of time complaining about the workload or moaning about the boss. So when there's a griping session going on, decide whether to join in or whether you'd really rather spend that time getting your work done. Don't make it so obvious that you make yourself unpopular with your workmates, of course – from time to time you can listen to them and nod, but don't add fuel to the fire and don't get sucked in.

Focus on one thing at a time

Lots of us try to do too many things at once, and that makes it hard to concentrate and work productively. Focus on one project at a time and try to ensure you are not disturbed – put your phone on voicemail and close your office door, if you can. Deal with interruptions by asking, 'Could you leave this with me?' or 'Let me give it some thought' – both a polite way of saying, 'Go away and leave me alone.'

Don't waste time in unproductive meetings

In meetings that take place towards the end of the day, you can often tell the people who have a family to get home to and the ones who don't. Those who don't (well, some of them) seem quite happy to waste hours arguing, nit-picking, rambling or going off the point, while those who do just want to get through the business quickly, get the decisions made and get the meeting over with.

If you feel as though you are spending your life in meetings, why not offer to chair them yourself so that you can make sure everyone keeps to the point and leaves on time? Or, if this isn't possible, perhaps you could arrange to attend the part of the meeting that relates to your work rather than the whole meeting.

Leave better voice-mail messages

Most of us waste a lot of time trying unsuccessfully to get hold of people on the phone. Experts recommend that if you are out of the office, you should leave a voice-mail message that tells callers exactly when you will be back at your desk. Just saying, 'I'm away from the office at the moment,' means they don't know when to call you back, so they are likely to leave a message, which means you will have to spend some of your time trying to get hold of them in return. Chances are they'll be out when you try to return their call. So leave a more informative message and you will get better responses from the people trying to call you – which saves everyone time.

Be prepared

If you have to go to appointments with people away from your workplace and you carry a diary around then, when you note down the appointment, at the same time make a note of the phone number of the person you are going to see. That way, if you do find you're running late or have to cancel, you will be able to quickly make a call to explain, without having to search for the person's contact details.

Take breaks

When you have a lot of work and you are under pressure, it can be tempting to work through your lunch hour. But fatigue can set in in the afternoon when your energy levels drop because you haven't eaten a proper lunch. Taking a break from your desk to move around or go for a walk and have something nutritious to eat is important – you'll feel fresher and work more productively for the rest of the day and get through the work sooner.

Use your energy wisely

During the day our energy levels fluctuate. If you have the kind of job where you are in control of your own workload, you can organise your day accordingly. For instance, you might find that you are fresher and have more energy in the mornings, so this is the best time for tackling tricky jobs that demand a lot of concentration or jobs that are more physically demanding.

Know when to call it a day

Are you a bit of a workaholic on the quiet? Do you always seem to have pressing deadlines, and do you find it hard to drag yourself away from your work at the end of the day? Remind yourself of the old adage: 'No one ever says on their deathbed: "I wish I'd spent more time at the office".'

If all else fails, put a screensaver on your computer that says: 'Go home'.

Chapter 7:
House like a bomb site?

Many a working mother could identify with the little girl who, when offered the part of Cinderella in the school play, turned it down after reading the script on the grounds that it involved too much housework in the first act.

When you go back to work after having a baby, the dilemma you face is this: more stuff to do around the house and less time to do it in.

How you deal with this is a very personal thing. Some people can happily live surrounded by clutter, oblivious to dust on the bookshelves and mucky fingerprints on the walls. Others are only content when every surface is gleaming and everything is in its place.

Most working mums are probably somewhere in between – a clean and tidy house is wonderful in theory, but it can be a struggle finding the time to do the basics of cooking meals and washing clothes, let alone anything like dusting or vacuuming.

When you live alone, or as a couple, it's not difficult to keep the place reasonably presentable. Between the years of student or flat-sharing squalor and the chaos that comes from having kids, there might even be a few years when you are quite house-proud. But when you have a baby every room rapidly fills up with baby equipment, food is flicked or smeared around your kitchen, nasty stains appear on the sofa, toys colonise the house and pieces of Lego litter the stairs. Suddenly your lovely flat or house starts to look a little the worse for wear, and having friends over means embarking on a frantic clear-up.

It will make life a lot easier if you can relax your standards for a few years, while the kids are young. Okay, let's be realistic

– until they leave home. If you work and you only have evenings and weekends at home, you really won't want to spend too many of those precious hours doing housework.

Here are a few tips to cut corners, save time and make life a bit easier.

Prioritise

Keep things in perspective – dust on the shelves and smears on the paintwork might be annoying, but are not actually a health hazard. When there isn't time to do everything, prioritise the tasks that affect your family's health and safety. That means jobs like fitting smoke detectors, putting in a stair gate if you have a baby about to start crawling, keeping your kitchen and food preparation surfaces and your toilets clean, and picking up anything from the floor or stairs that could trip someone up. Oh, and preparing meals, of course.

Enlist help

Hopefully your partner, if you have one, is already pulling his weight (if he's not, see Chapter 10). As your children get older, try to get them into good habits. Even toddlers can learn to put their own toys away in the toy box before bed. Older children might be able to help you with some of the chores, especially if you are one of those scarily efficient mothers who can manage to persuade them that it's fun.

It might take twice as long to do the task with their help, but, with luck, as they grow up they will get more competent and it will save you time in the long run.

Possible tasks for older kids include: hanging out washing, cleaning the car, dusting and polishing, raking and gathering up autumn leaves from the path or garden. They sometimes enjoy a bit of food preparation – washing vegetables or salad leaves, buttering bread or making sandwiches – and if you have two kids or more you could have a rota for regular jobs like laying the table and washing up or stacking the dishwasher. Think it can't be done? Well, you could always try bribery!

Don't be a hoarder

The more stuff you have in your home, the harder it is to get it looking tidy. Being surrounded by clutter is stressful. So have a good clear-out every so often, and be brutal.

Experts suggest that you look at every item, from clothes and sports goods to books and pictures, and ask yourself: 'Do I use this?' and 'Do I love it?' If the answer to both questions is no, throw it away, give it to someone else or donate it to charity. Let it have a new home with someone else who will love it!

It can be tempting to keep too much from the past. Experts say that if you find you are clinging on to things that reflect who you used to be – clothes that don't fit you any more, or hobbies you gave up long ago – it's better to get rid of them and make space for the person you are today.

Put the toys out of sight

Even when the kids are finally in bed, it can be hard to relax in a room that's still strewn with toys. Have a storage box in the living room so that it's easy to chuck the toys into the box and out of sight for the rest of the evening.

Having a sea of toys just encourages a child to throw them around and it makes it difficult for him to focus and concentrate on one toy or game. So instead of having all his toys out all the time, keep some tucked away in a cupboard and bring out different ones every few weeks – apart from giving you a tidier home, this will help your child get more fun out of his toys because they don't become overfamiliar.

Encourage your children to get rid of old toys as they are given new ones – it prevents your house from filling up with toys and gets them into good habits. Explain how giving the toys to a charity shop could help other children who are not as lucky as they are.

Save on time spent sorting washing

Have two laundry baskets, one for white clothes and the other for coloured. Train all the members of the family (including older children) to put their dirty clothes in the right basket – with shirt-sleeves unrolled and socks opened out rather than in a tight ball.

Save on ironing time

If you hate ironing, buy easy-iron shirts rather than cotton. Hang shirts to dry on a plastic coat hanger as soon as you get them out of the washing machine and you might get away without having to iron them at all. If you always wear a jacket with your shirt and time is short, just iron the fronts, not the whole garment.

Everything in its place

To save hours searching for house keys and door keys, have a hook by the front door where you always hang them as soon as you come in. (But make sure thieves can't see them and hook them out through the letter box with a long implement – it has been known!)

If you and your children borrow books or tapes from the library, have a special place in the house where you keep them all whenever you're not using them. It saves hours of hunting round the house for them on the day they're due back.

Encourage tidy habits

It could take you years, but try to get everyone in the family in the habit of putting things away when they have finished with them. Have a family 'lost property' box into which you can drop any odd socks, shoes, parts of toys or anything else you find lying around. Get family members to claim them, and anything suitable that's not claimed after a few weeks can be sent to the charity shop.

doesn't cost much and it gets you round the store in half the time.

⊙ More and more farmers' markets are springing up all over the UK. Okay, maybe strolling around the market for fresh bread, cheese, fruit, meat and veg isn't any quicker than zapping round Tesco, but farmers' markets have a fun atmosphere and good quality produce and can make a nice change, especially if you have to take the kids shopping with you. Find your nearest one at www.farmersmarkets.net.

> ### Carol says:
>
> I do quite a lot of supermarket shopping late at night – my supermarket is open twenty-four hours and as long as there is someone else at home with the kids, it's a good idea to scoot round while the store is quiet. I find taking three children round the supermarket quite stressful!

Lunchboxes

Lunchboxes are the bane of many a working mother's life. In theory you can make up a week's supply of sandwiches in one go and freeze them for the whole family to take to the nursery, school, office or factory. This could well be a labour-saving idea, but not many of us relish the idea of putting aside a half a day at the weekend for sandwich-making. Most of us end up doing it each morning, somewhere between feeding the cat and finding the gym kit.

Here are some lunchbox suggestions:

⊙ As sandwich fillings, low-fat peanut butter, low-fat cheese or soft cheese spread, fish (e.g. mackerel or tuna) canned in brine.

⊙ Pieces of carrot, cucumber or celery, or pitta bread to dip into hummus, taramasalata or other dips; cherry tomatoes; strips of green or red pepper.

⊙ Oat cakes or muesli bars.

⊙ Yoghurt or fromage frais.

⊙ Fruit and dried fruit such as raisins and dried apricots.

Keep stocked up

Having some basic items in the house means you can always have something to hand to rustle up a meal from, even if you haven't managed to get to the supermarket for fresh meat, fish or vegetables.

Apart from baked beans (where would we be without them?), how about:

⊙ Tins of tuna (to make tuna pasta bake, mix with pasta sauce, cooked pasta and a tin of sweet corn, sprinkle with cheese and cook in the oven).

⊙ Canned beans (such as pinto beans, flageolet beans and cannellini beans) and chickpeas; or puy lentils, which don't have to be soaked before cooking.

⊙ Tins of canned tomatoes and tomato purée (use with the beans and flavour with spices to make a spicy bean stew).

⊙ Rice, noodles, pasta and couscous.

⊙ Dried onions and dried mushrooms to add to casseroles and stews.

⊙ Eggs – keep some in the fridge and you will always be able to produce a quick omelette or scrambled eggs in a matter of minutes.

⊙ Chorizos and other long-life sausages, for casseroles, pizzas and so on.

⊙ Tins of mackerel in tomato sauce – mackerel on toast with a side salad is quick and nutritious.

Save time in the kitchen

⊙ When you do have time to cook a meal, such as a chicken casserole, beef stew or fish pie, make twice the quantity and freeze half of it so that you can have an effortless dinner on another occasion. (Remember that you may need to increase the cooking time given in the recipe when you cook larger quantities.)

⊙ If you are making your own baby foods, freeze small quantities of the purée in ice-cube trays to use later. Once it's frozen you can remove the cubes from the tray and store them in the freezer in plastic bags.

⊙ Speed up the cooking time of baked potatoes by pushing a metal skewer through the middle of each one.

⊙ Keep your non-perishable foodstuffs like pasta, rice and raisins in transparent containers so that you can see at a glance how much is left.

⊙ Scrubbing the grill pan has to be one of the worst jobs going. If you know you aren't going to have time to do it, line the grill pan with kitchen foil curved up at the side to catch the juices, and replace as necessary.

⊙ If you work part-time and you have more time in the morning than the evening, you could buy a slow cooker. That way, you can prepare the evening meal in the morning and leave it to cook all day with no risk of burning – and hey presto, when you walk in the door after work, the meal is all ready to serve up.

⊙ Teach older kids how to wash up or stack the dishwasher. Get them to help you set up a rota for them with jobs like laying the table, clearing away after a meal and wiping down the kitchen table. Change the jobs round every week so they don't get bored.

⊙ Use convenience foods with a clear conscience – you are not Superwoman!

Carol says:

When the kids go to parties they often come back full of sweets and ice cream at about five o'clock and don't feel like eating a proper meal. I usually let them have a bowl of cereal or something instead – I think that's all right once in a while.

Meals with child appeal

When there's time to spare, older kids like to help prepare meals – and they are guaranteed to eat something they've had a hand in making. Here are a few ideas:

⊙ Buy ready-made pizza bases and jars of pizza topping. Start by getting the kids to spread the pizza topping or tomato purée over the base, sprinkle with grated cheese, then add whatever you have to hand – they can decorate it with slices of salami, strips of ham, sliced mushrooms, tomatoes, green or red peppers, sweet corn and so on. While it's in the oven, get them to clear up the bomb site that was your kitchen.

⊙ If you have more than one child – or if they have friends round – get a chicken nugget production line going. Make your own by cutting up boneless chicken pieces into small strips. Child 1 coats a strip of chicken with flour; child 2 then dips it into beaten egg; finally, child 3 coats it with breadcrumbs or herby stuffing mix. When all the strips are done, shallow-fry them and serve them with potatoes and vegetables or inside a pitta pocket with salad.

⊙ Let them wash and chop the fruit for a fruit salad.

⊙ They can wash and prepare crudités, such as strips of carrot, celery, red and green peppers, to dip in hummus or other dips.

⊙ They can make sandwiches.

Carol says:

My kids' favourite is something we call sausage monsters – it's a mound of mashed potato with sausages, cut in half, sticking out of it at odd angles and surrounded by a pool of gravy. They love it because it looks so weird.

They also like macaroni cheese, which is really quick to make and good for them.

Each of our children has been through a phase of not eating anything. It's taken a while, but we've learned not to get too hung up about it or try to force them to eat.

Easy entertaining

When guests are coming to dinner, are you so frazzled by a day of hard graft over a hot stove that you snarl at anyone who dares to cross the kitchen threshold (until the doorbell rings, of course, and they arrive and it's smiles all round)? Have you ever found that, by the time the meal is finally over and you slump into an armchair, you have trouble keeping your eyes open? You need to make entertaining a bit easier on yourself.

⊙ Don't agonise over the menu or feel that you must spend two days marinating the beef. Simple, informal food is 'in' for dinner parties right now.

⊙ Does cooking the dinner and cleaning the house all in the same weekend seem too much like hard work? If you choose something like a casserole you can cook it one weekend, freeze it, and serve it the next weekend. Or cook it the evening before, when the kids are in bed, refrigerate it overnight and reheat it ready for the dinner party. Some casseroles and stews improve when the flavours infuse overnight.

⊙ If you are inviting another two couples over, why not suggest that each couple brings a dish instead of a bottle of wine or chocolates? If one brings a starter and the other a dessert, you only have one course to prepare. You can return the favour at your next get-together.

⊙ If a group of you meets up regularly, you could suggest that everyone chips in to have a takeaway meal delivered. Your friends, especially if they have young children too, may be just as happy not to have to cook when it's their turn to be the hosts.

⊙ Most supermarkets have a 'luxury' range, or try your local delicatessen – if you have run out of time to cook, a bit of gourmet shopping could be the answer to your prayers.

⊙ Good friends just want to see you and enjoy your company – so chill out! No one cares whether you made that sauce yourself or bought it from Marks & Spencer.

Carol says:

When you are entertaining friends with kids in the summertime, barbecues are easy to do. Men always like cooking on barbecues! You can prepare a lot of the salads and other stuff beforehand, and kids will always eat a sausage from the barbecue.

Dead easy dinner-party dishes

Starters

⊙ Serve slices of halloumi cheese, browned under the grill, with some salad leaves. Grilled goat's cheese is great too – pick the small round ones with a rind, slice in half horizontally and put under the grill, cut side up. Serve with salad, a blob of cranberry sauce and a sprinkling of hazelnuts.

⊙ Serve a selection of cold meats and cheese from the deli, drizzled with olive oil and arranged on a plate with olives.

Crusty bread and dips from the deli is another simple but delicious idea.

Main courses

⊙ For a speedy but delicious pasta dish, sauté some sliced onions and mushrooms. Mix these with cooked pasta and prawns or smoked salmon cut into small pieces. Heat the whole lot together with some soft herb and garlic cheese, which will melt into a lovely garlicky sauce.

⊙ Salmon – a breeze to prepare and very tasty, served grilled, baked in the oven in foil or in a sauce.

Desserts

⊙ Buy a pavlova base, fill it with whipped cream and top with fresh fruit (or defrost a packet of mixed forest fruits and arrange those on top).

⊙ Treat them to a chocolate fondue – pre-prepare a selection of sliced fruits and biscotti biscuits, then you can make the fondue at the table while you chat. Let it stand for a few minutes to thicken before everyone starts dipping.

⊙ Give them a gorgeous chocolate gateau or fruit tart from your nearest patisserie.

Carol says:

I find that ice cream with smashed-up mini-Crunchie bars always goes down well at a dinner party – break them up in a plastic bag with a rolling pin, then sprinkle it over the ice cream.

Chapter 9:
Your money – and where it goes

Starting a family is a momentous decision and totting up how much it will cost may seem decidedly unromantic. But having your first baby involves major expense and is likely to affect your finances in a big way for years to come.

Sitting down to do a little financial planning (preferably before you even get pregnant) will reduce the risk of money worries spoiling this exciting time in your life.

As the first step in your budget plan, you need to know exactly what you spend your pre-baby money on.

Just what do you spend your money on?

Gather together all your household bills, bank and credit card statements and so on, and get ready to look at exactly how much you are spending – and where it's going.

⊙ List all your regular monthly outgoings: rent or mortgage repayments, insurance premiums, life assurance, gas, electricity and phone bills, Internet charges, council tax, pension contributions and so on. If there are certain bills that you pay quarterly or annually, write down how much this works out at per month.

⊙ Estimate how much you spend on food at the supermarket each month and write this down.

⊙ Now think of the expenses relating to your car: tax, insurance, regular servicing, petrol and AA or RAC membership. Again, estimate how much these work out at on a monthly basis, and add this sum to your list.

⊙ If you or your partner uses public transport to get to work, add on the cost of your fares each month.

⊙ Tot up any other payments or subscriptions you make, such as your television licence, your professional association, regular donations to charity, and add the monthly average of these to your list.

⊙ Note down an amount that you think would cover house maintenance and repairs. When you have worked out roughly how much per year, divide by twelve to give you a monthly average.

⊙ Now think about all the extras you spend your money on: expenses such as birthday presents, Christmas presents, haircuts, leg waxes, cosmetics, dentist's bills, magazines and so on. Estimate how much you spend on things like this and add a monthly average to your list.

⊙ Work out how much you and your partner spend on clothes and shoes, as a monthly average.

⊙ Finally, work out how much you spend on average, each month, on entertainment, leisure, gym or sports and eating out. If an annual holiday is a must for you, work out how much this costs and add in a monthly sum for this too.

⊙ Now add up your total monthly outgoings.

The second stage is to work out how much money you have coming in: add up your salary and your partner's (if you have a partner), and any other income you have.

Hopefully your income comfortably exceeds your outgoings.

How things change with a baby

Now let's look at what extra costs, and financial help, you can expect when you are having a baby.

Baby costs

You will need savings to buy some essential items before the baby is born, such as a pushchair, crib, car seat and clothes. Later on there are more clothes and more equipment to buy, such as safety gates and highchairs. If, in your baby's first year, you were to buy everything you needed from somewhere like Mothercare, opting for the most basic versions of everything, you would still get no change from £1,000 – and that's without buying toys or allowing for running costs of nappies, milk or food.

If this has left you in shock, don't panic – there are ways of cutting the cost.

⊙ Grandparents often like to chip in; friends and relatives will lend or pass on their outgrown baby equipment; and you are bound to be given baby outfits and toys when your baby arrives, and at Christmas.

⊙ You could also look for bargains in baby equipment in the small ads of your local paper or contact your local branch of the National Childbirth Trust (see page 173) to see if they have a nearly-new sale coming up.

⊙ Never use a child car seat that has been involved in an accident or buy a second-hand car seat, as there could have been some damage to the protective structure that is not visible. It may be best to buy a new mattress too – some cot death researchers believe that babies who routinely sleep on a mattress previously used by another child may be at increased risk of cot death.

⊙ Babies are expensive to run – disposable nappies alone will cost you at least £20 a month. If you are bottle-feeding, you'll need to buy formula milk. And don't forget that babies have the annoying habit of outgrowing their entire wardrobe every couple of months.

⊙ You will find that you are running the washing machine more frequently than you ever thought possible.

- By far the biggest expense comes when you return to work – the cost of childcare varies a lot but is likely to eat up a large part of your income. See Chapter 4 for a guide to the costs of different kinds of childcare.

- You may even find that you have to run an extra car because you need to take your baby to the child minder or nursery before work.

- Depending on how long you plan to take off work and how generous your company is, you may have to budget for several months on a lower income than usual while you are on Ordinary Maternity Leave and possibly no income at all on Additional Maternity Leave. If your partner is going to take paternity leave, take this into account as well (see page 164).

- Chapter 14 will tell you how much maternity pay you can expect – but you may find that your company offers a deal that is more generous than the statutory minimum. For instance, you may remain on full pay for all or part of your Ordinary Maternity Leave. Some continue to pay women a full salary, on condition that they return to work afterwards. If you are in this situation, even if you intend to go back to work, it makes sense to try to save the money if you possibly can. If you spend it and then can't bear the thought of going back, you will have the added headache of having to repay money that you haven't got.

- The good news is that you will spend less in total on going out, because (here comes the bad news) babies are bad for your social life. And if you do ever manage to get it together to go somewhere, the cost of a night out shoots up when you have to pay a baby-sitter.

Financial help for parents

Child benefit

Up to April 2007, this is £17.45 a week for your first child and

£11.70 a week for subsequent children. Every family is entitled to this, regardless of income, and the exact amount changes in the Budget each year.

Start claiming it when you have registered your baby's birth (you need the birth certificate to make your claim). You may be given a claim form but if not, ring the Child Benefit Centre on 0845 3021444.

It can be paid straight into a bank, building society, Post Office or National Savings account that accepts Direct Payment, or you may be sent a cheque to cash at the Post Office.

Tax Credits

Child Tax Credit is for families with at least one child. It has a 'family element' payable to a family responsible for a child, and this is paid at a higher rate to families with at least one child under the age of one. There is also a 'child element' payable for each child that you are responsible for. The Working Tax Credit is for people who are in paid work, which includes a 'childcare element' paid to help working parents who have to spend money on childcare. The amount you receive depends on your annual income, the number of children you have and the amount you pay for childcare. Claim on-line at www.taxcredits. inlandrevenue.gov.uk or phone the information helpline on 0845 300 3900.

Benefits for parents on a low income

If you or your partner get a low-income benefit or tax credit you may be eligible for a Sure Start Maternity Grant. This is a one-off payment to help with the cost of things for a new baby. There are other grants and interest-free loans for people claiming benefits – ask at your local social security office. If you are on a low income and you are a lone parent you might be able to get Income Support.

Where to find out more about benefits

The Department for Work and Pensions is responsible for a range of benefits and services for families.

For guides and leaflets on social security and benefits, contact your local social security office (see the display advert under Benefits Agency in the business numbers section of the phone book) or Jobcentre Plus.

Summing up your finances

Taking all the above factors into account, look at your sums again to see what your financial situation is going to be like when you go back to work. This exercise should have given you a good idea of how you will manage financially, both over your maternity leave period and afterwards, when you go back to work.

However you look at it, babies are expensive little creatures – and that's even before they start demanding ballet classes, riding lessons, Barbie dolls, bikes and trainers. But you won't begrudge a penny of it. Let's face it – what else could you possibly spend your money on that would enrich your life in so many wonderful ways?

When income minus expenditure equals ouch!

If it looks as though you are going to run into difficulties, think about where you could cut costs to make ends meet. Rather than trying to save small amounts, here are three ways you could save substantial amounts of money. Unfortunately, only the first is painless.

⊙ Find out whether you could get a better deal by switching your mortgage to another lender offering a lower rate of interest. You could be surprised at how much you can save on your monthly repayments. Transferring your credit card balance to another card could also save you a lot in interest.

⊙ Missing out on your annual holiday might seem drastic but

it's probably one of the biggest outgoings on your list. You could think about house swapping with friends – you still get a change of scene, but it costs next to nothing.

⊙ Running a car (or even two) is an expensive business. If you live and work somewhere where you could manage on public transport instead, selling your car could save you lots of money at a stroke. You can have your weekly shopping delivered if you order via the Internet and, for the times when you really can't do without a car, like holidays, you hire one.

The true cost of getting to work

The Telework Association quotes the example of an average commuter who works forty hours a week and spends another four hours travelling. The average household expenditure per car per week is around £50 and it costs around £1,000 for an annual city centre parking ticket. In total this costs £3,500 a year. Which means the commuter is spending a quarter of his or her time either getting to work or earning the money to pay for the journey.

The worst case scenario is 'Didcot manager' who runs a car to get to the station and then travels to central London by rail. He/she earns £26,000 a year. Suppose Didcot manager spends 14 hours commuting in addition to working 43 hours a week. Taking into account the time spent travelling, and after paying tax and deducting money to run the car, pay for parking and rail tickets, Didcot manager's 'true' hourly pay rate is – rather startlingly – less than £5 per hour. (And that's even without deducting childcare costs.)

The Telework Association points out that Didcot manager would actually be better off, work fewer hours, be healthier and have a better quality of life by taking a lower-paid job closer to home.

Do you have debts?

If you are in debt, going through the exercise above and finding out how much is left at the end of the month will give you an idea of how much you have available (if anything) to repay your debt and over how long a period. Here are a few final suggestions:

- ⊙ If you have big debts, don't put your head in the sand and hope they will go away. The sooner you tackle debts, the better.

- ⊙ Prioritise your debts and pay off the ones that will result in severe penalties if you don't pay them back – such as having your house repossessed or your electricity cut off.

- ⊙ If you're not sure what to do, seek advice from your local Citizens' Advice Bureau.

- ⊙ If you have a large credit card debt, consider transferring it to another card that charges lower (or no) interest for the first six months – and then try hard to pay off the debt in that time.

Chapter 10:
You and your man

National statistics show that in Great Britain in the year 2000, 18 per cent of dependent children lived in lone-mother families, 80 per cent in 'couple families' and just 2 per cent in lone-father families.

This chapter is about mothers and fathers in 'couple families'.

Over half of all divorces occur in the first ten years of marriage and, whether a couple is married or living together, there's no doubt that the arrival of a child puts pressure on a relationship. It's wonderful, but it does change everything – your feelings, your finances, your home, your social life, your relationship, your sex life and even (or especially) what you and your partner argue about.

In the face of these changes in your lifestyle, the kind of relationship you want – in an ideal world – is one in which you and your partner are pulling together rather than in different directions. You co-operate. You're on the same side. You support each other, through good times and bad. Trouble is, lots of things can get in the way.

When the baby arrives

For some new mothers, having a baby is a bit like falling in love all over again. You gaze into your baby's eyes adoringly, can't stop touching him, think about him all the time and can't bear to be parted for a second. It's intense and overwhelming. No wonder some new dads feel sidelined – maybe even a tad jealous, deep down. The family dynamics have changed overnight, in a big way. For a while, your man isn't going to be number one any more – and some men find it hard to adjust.

What's more, the first few weeks with a new baby can be emotionally and physically exhausting for both of you. Get him to tell you how he's feeling – men often feel they can't share their worries about pregnancy, birth or the new baby because they are supposed to be the strong ones.

In the early days after your baby is born, when you are regaling your friends with stories about the birth and everyone is cooing over the baby, congratulating you and showering you with flowers, the father's role usually comes down to making the tea.

Dads may not be able to breast-feed but they can do many other useful things: cuddle babies, bath them, give a bottle, change nappies and rock them to sleep or walk them up and down when they are crying. They can cook, wash up and do the other household chores and generally be supportive, helpful and understanding.

Paternity leave

Dads are now entitled to two weeks' Statutory Paternity Leave around the birth (or the placement of an adopted child) to care for the baby and support the mother. They are eligible if they have worked for their employer continuously for 26 weeks into the 15th week before the baby is due. They can take either one week or two consecutive weeks' leave and the leave must be taken within 56 days of the baby's birth (or, if the baby is born early, up to 56 days after the expected week of the birth). Most employees will be entitled to Statutory Paternity Pay from their employers, which at the time of writing is £108.85 a week (or 90 per cent of average earnings if this is less than £108.85). They have to inform their employers that they want paternity leave by the 15th week before the baby is expected, saying when the baby is due, whether they want to take one or two weeks' leave and when they want their leave to start.

Many men choose not to take paternity leave – perhaps

because they can't afford it or because they feel the entire stock market would collapse if they weren't around for two weeks. According to a survey by government news portal YouGov in 2006, only 37 per cent of fathers took the full statutory two weeks' paid leave and 58 per cent took less than a week. But if your man can take paternity leave, it's a chance for you to learn about your baby together. And it means he can start helping – right from the beginning.

Don't hog the baby!

Have you ever caught yourself tutting as he fumbles to change or bath the baby? If he's dressing the baby, does he always feel he has to ask you what the baby should wear? If he offers to make up a bottle, do you say, 'No, I'll do it,' or hover over him anxiously? This kind of thing makes a new father feel that, as far as the baby is concerned, the woman is the expert and he will never do it quite as well as her.

> In 1999 the *Journal of Marriage and the Family* studied 622 dual-earner families and noted that some women discourage the father's involvement with the baby 'by redoing tasks, criticising, creating unbending standards or demeaning their efforts'. It calls this behaviour 'maternal gatekeeping'.

Is it any wonder that some men become demoralised and end up doing less and less with the baby?

Cheer him on. He may not do things exactly the way you would, but how will men learn to look after babies if women don't let them near?

Another good reason for encouraging him is that, if you are going back to work, you won't be able to do everything yourself even if you want to. Involving your partner right from the start sets a pattern and means he will be more confident about sharing the care later on, when both of you are working. He will discover the pleasure of looking after and playing with the baby and enjoy the closeness it brings. It will also make your life as a working mother easier. Makes sense, doesn't it?

Carol says:

I have seen this 'maternal gatekeeping' in friends when we have been on holiday with them. Before, I have thought, 'That guy never does anything with those children.' But after spending a few days away with the family you can see that it's not that he won't do anything, it's that she doesn't let him do anything. She thinks he's incapable or makes him feel incapable. Maybe early on he made a mess of something and she has never let him do anything ever again. Once I realised, I felt terrible for judging the relationship the wrong way!

Delegation

Lots of advice is given to mothers, especially working mothers, about the importance of 'delegating' household tasks and child-care to their partners. The trouble with this is that it presupposes that all the responsibility for household tasks and childcare is yours – and that if your man helps out, it is as a favour to you and should earn him your undying gratitude.

In fact, as any 'new man' worth his salt realises, the house and children are just as much his responsibility as yours. Traditional notions of motherhood had women thinking that all the unpaid work was theirs, whether or not they were holding down a demanding full-time paid job as well. The world has moved on. Try to cultivate the spirit of equal partnership, in which your partner participates in the domestic and family work because that is only fair and just.

Danger: men at work

One difficulty that could stand in the way of the 'new man' doing his fair share is his working hours. Like you, he may long for more time with his kids – but the demands of his job or career may mean that this isn't always easy.

On average, women's working hours drop dramatically once they have children, but men's working hours increase. For women, for a number of reasons, it's easier to go part-time or reduce hours; but in many households men feel that this option isn't open to them and they are stuck in the role of being the main provider.

As an individual family you may be able to arrange your working lives so that you share the childcare and the paid work equally, if that's what you both want. But for society as a whole, there's a long way to go. The choice that women face when it comes to family life and professional success is not so stark for men, but it is there nonetheless. If men want to spend time with their families, if they want to be dad rather than just the breadwinner, real changes in the labour market and in working cultures are needed. Women may not have it all, but men don't either.

Dads matter – and we should make sure they know it. If a man knows that his partner and their kids really value having him at home and that he's important to the family, he's more likely to hurry home to have some time with them before bedtime instead of staying in his office until nine o'clock at night.

In a 2002 survey by the Chartered Institute of Personnel and Development, nearly half of people who worked over 48 hours a week said their long working hours caused arguments in the home, while one in three felt guilty about missing out as their children grew up.

The partners of the long-hours workers were also questioned: 43 per cent said they were fed up with having to shoulder most of the domestic burden, and 70 per cent said that the long-hours worker was sometimes too tired even to hold a conversation.

More than half of the long-hours workers said they had a problem with their sex life, with nearly a third reporting that it was affected by work-related tiredness and 14 per cent suffering from reduced libido.

Planning

Before you go back to work, you can never really know what life is going to be like as a working mother. Even though it's pretty difficult to imagine, it's a good idea to sit down and try to plan how you will organise things.

⊙ Who will get your baby or child to the child minder or nursery?

⊙ Who will do the shopping, the washing, the cooking, the cleaning, the ironing?

⊙ Who will take responsibility for making sure the bills get paid?

⊙ If you have older children, who will take them to their after-school and weekend activities and make sure they do their homework?

Of course, you need some flexibility and you'll find that some of your arrangements buckle under the pressure of day-to-day events, but at least if you have some semblance of a plan it's a good start. And it makes it clear to your partner that one person (i.e. you) won't be able to manage everything.

As well as having a grand plan, you'll probably find you need to sit down on a Sunday evening with the calendar and your diaries to plan any special arrangements for the coming week.

Relate has the following advice:

Don't be afraid to ask for help – your partner and children aren't mind-readers. Most people respond well if asked pleasantly. Don't snap, nag or leave asking until you are at the end of your tether. Make sharing the load an accepted part of daily life, rather than a problem which always causes a row. Decide together who will do what. Allow for preferences – your partner may hate ironing, but be quite happy to shop or cook.

Carol says:

You both have to appreciate that the responsibility for the children is shared and you shouldn't feel that you have to take it all on yourself. Talk it over between the two of you before you go back to work – don't simply assume he will help. My husband Alex is pretty good. Before we even had children we discussed my working and he knows that without my job our life would be very different – just as it would without his job.

'You owe me ten lie-ins'

Some couples, struggling with the demands of life with a baby or toddler, fall into the trap of operating a kind of points system. He spends an hour in the pub after work one night, so she demands an hour of looking round the shops on Saturday. She has a night out with friends or a trip to the hairdresser, so he feels he is owed a couple of hours playing squash on Sunday morning.

On one level it makes sense, of course. You've lost the flexibility that you had, as a childless couple, to go out when you want, so there has to be some give and take if each of you is to get any time at all to do your own thing.

If sex is becoming just a distant memory for you, you are not alone. It might be because of sheer exhaustion, lack of time, resentment, depression, no longer feeling desirable or even, subconsciously, no longer seeing the point of sex once you have had a baby. It can be hard to feel attracted to a partner who never helps. And of course sharing your bed with a baby or toddler is the kiss of death to passion. Whatever the reason, it's easy to get out of the habit of making love.

If you've practically given up on sex, think about why this has happened and work out what would make you want it again or what would make it possible. This may mean sending the kids to grandma's overnight, some new sexy underwear, a lock on your bedroom door if you are afraid of being interrupted, a late-afternoon nap so that you can stay awake later in the evening, or a romantic night out (hopefully not with a new man).

At certain times in your life, sex happens spontaneously but at other times you may have to be a bit more proactive. Experts sometimes advise that, when motivation is lacking, women should deliberately schedule time for sex. The theory is that, like most things, if it's in your diary you'll do it, and that you will enjoy it once you get going – in fact, they say the more sex you have, the more you want it!

No one to baby-sit?

Spending time together is important even if, at the end of a night out, you fall asleep the moment your head touches the pillow. But if nights out with your partner are few and far between because you can't find a baby-sitter, how about setting up a baby-sitting circle?

You arrange it with a group of five or six friends who all have children and issue everyone with a certain number of tokens and a list of everyone's contact details. When you need a baby-sitter, you phone anyone on the list and see if they are available.

At the end of an evening's baby-sitting you pay in tokens – each token represents half an hour's baby-sitting (two tokens per half-hour after midnight). To earn tokens and stay in credit, each person has to do a certain amount of baby-sitting – but this doesn't have to be with the same person who baby-sat for her, it can be anyone in the circle.

Granted, you have to do some baby-sitting in return – but sitting in someone else's house, with someone else's kids in bed upstairs and no chores to do, can be surprisingly relaxing. You might even find yourself getting round to one of those little jobs you've been putting off for ages, like writing a letter or arranging your photos in albums.

If you don't know any friends with children who would want to join in, contact your local branch of the National Childbirth Trust (see page 173) and get to know other mums that way. You could even arrange a reunion of your antenatal group and put the idea to them.

Arguments

When both of you are tired and perhaps feeling stressed, you have less patience with each other and tempers fray more quickly.

According to the partnership counselling organisation Relate, these are the main subjects that couples argue about:

- Money.
- Sex.
- Untidiness.
- Disciplining children.
- Housework.
- Parents and friends.

And there are four highly destructive patterns of rows:

⊙ Stonewalling: total withdrawal and refusal to discuss the issue. Partner feels unvalued and unheard.

⊙ Criticism: commenting negatively on the other's behaviour, over and above the current problem. Partner feels attacked and threatened.

⊙ Contempt: sneering, belligerence or sarcasm. Partner feels humiliated and belittled.

⊙ Defensiveness: aggressively defending and justifying self to partner. Partner feels attacked. Row escalates.

Relate advises that you aim for the 'win-win' style of disagreeing, in which partners outline their own needs and listen to each other's needs, then talk flexibly about solutions that give each of them enough of what they want.

And if it seems too difficult to get your partner to talk about changing the way you argue, says Relate, go ahead and start changing anyway – your partner's reactions will alter in response to yours.

One Plus One, an organisation which researches into what makes relationships work, has looked at parental conflict and concludes that *how* parents argue is what matters to children. Children are unlikely to be troubled if their parents manage and resolve disputes effectively. It could even help them to learn how to deal with conflict themselves in later life. But children are at risk of behavioural and/or emotional problems when disagreements between their parents are:

⊙ Frequent and intense.

⊙ Full of aggression.

⊙ About the child.

⊙ Concealed as quiet contempt or hostility.

⊙ Ended abruptly by one partner withdrawing or storming out.

So there you have it – if you must argue, at least do it right. And make sure you aren't blaming each other for things that are no one's fault.

Finally, you can be comforted by the thought that, even if you argue a lot early on in your relationship, things may change as you get older and wiser and perhaps more tolerant of each other.

Reflecting on his 21st wedding anniversary and the changes that having children brought to the relationship, Observer columnist and father of four Phil Hogan wrote:

'Marriage at its finest is a noble expression of compromise, but of course it can only be made to balance by one of you realising that men will never do their precise share of the housework because only women know precisely how much there is. For his part, the man of the house might lower his expectations with regard to the location, frequency and spontaneity of sexual intercourse.

'Admittedly there are bound to be skirmishes about how to share the sleep (unlike housework, there is less of this to go round) and you still have room in your lives for wondering aloud who has left the empty toilet roll on the holder, but it soon becomes apparent that the big battles have been won or lost. You can't go out any more, or at least not together (and it does take two drunks to make a drunken argument) and – more important – you now have a common enemy. In our house at least, most of the bickering and domestic violence these days comes from the children. It seems only natural and right that it is they who will keep the sacred flame of rancour alive. For us the war is over.'

Mary says:

When my husband and I got married, my dad gave a speech at our wedding. He said that, in a marriage, what you give out, you get back: kind words will be met with kind words, harsh words with harsh words. And it's true. When I am tired or stressed and I snap at my husband, he snaps back. But when I am warm and affectionate to him, he responds in the same way to me.

Why listening matters

Even though we may have chosen working motherhood, it doesn't mean it is always going to be wonderful. There may be times when work is going badly or the sheer hard daily grind gets on top of you. For many women, talking about our feelings is one of the most important ways we cope when we are finding things difficult. Sometimes talking about what we are going through can really make us feel better – even if there's nothing anyone can do to help.

The trouble is that most men don't operate that way. Men are notorious for not being good at talking about feelings and may not understand a woman's need to talk about her feelings.

If you talk to your partner about how hard you are finding things or how tired you feel, he is likely to take it as a criticism of himself and to think you are implying that it's his fault. Or he may think that he should somehow be able to solve the problem for you, and feel bad that he can't. He may get defensive, or say things like: 'Well, you wanted to go back to work – you can't complain,' or 'What do you want me to do about it?'

The solution is easy: tell him that you are not blaming him for whatever it is (if that is the case) and you know there may be nothing he can do, but that it makes you feel much better anyway when you can talk to him like this. He may not understand why or how it has helped, but that doesn't matter as long as he knows you appreciate him for listening!

Friends

You will probably find, as many new parents do, that you seem to gravitate towards friends who also have children. Unlike your childless friends, they won't look at you with pity as they watch you desperately trying to comfort a colicky baby while hosting a dinner party, and their jaws won't drop at the sight of your previously immaculate flat, now given over completely to baby equipment. Nor will they watch with appalled fascination as your toddler upends a bowl of soup all over his head or wince when your three-year-old charges into the room, yelling.

In short, friends who have kids understand – they are going through the same thing and they are only too familiar with the chaos of child-rearing. What's even better is if they have children a bit older than yours and can tell you what fresh horror to expect from the next phase of parenthood.

When you can share the ups and downs of working parenthood with friends, it helps to put things into perspective – yesterday's work or childcare disasters have a habit of becoming today's laugh-out-loud dinner-party anecdotes.

Carol says:

We get together with friends for lunch at weekends because while our kids are playing together we can actually have a conversation. Our three often argue among themselves but when other children are around, they play really well with them.

Chapter 11:
Lone working mums

Looking after a baby without the support of a partner is hard, and to combine this with working is a real achievement. Many women do it successfully, to their immense credit.

In the year 2000, one in four of all families with dependent children was headed by a lone parent, according to the Office of National Statistics.

A government research report asked lone parents about the best and worst things about their situation.

Asked what were the best things, 60 per cent said that you are your own boss and have independence; 15 per cent said peace of mind; 10 per cent said it was having more time for the children and/or yourself.

Asked about the worst things, 48 per cent said loneliness; 45 per cent said financial difficulties; 8 per cent said that children need a father and mother.

If loneliness is a problem for you, then as well as the other suggestions for meeting friends that are given in this book, you could meet other single parents through Gingerbread, which has a network of local self-help groups running social events and outings for parents and their kids. The organisation also has an advice line offering confidential advice on issues like finance, housing and family law (see contact details on page 171). Its website has an e-mail discussion list and a chat room so you can exchange news and views with other single parents without even leaving the house.

Marlene says:

Going to work means that I have got money in my pocket and that I am not with my daughter twenty-four hours a day. I don't get much time to myself, there's no time to relax. But I do enjoy being with my daughter and I'm happy to be the one making all the decisions.

As well as working part-time, I am studying for a degree. I don't manage to do much work on my essays and assignments at night because I am tired, so I do that mostly at weekends. But I'm a fighter – I will see it through.

The National Council for One Parent Families (see page 174) also gives information and advice to parents bringing up children on their own.

If finances are a problem, these organisations will be able to advise you on whether you are claiming all the help you are entitled to, such as tax credits.

Without someone else around to share everything that's involved in bringing up a child and looking after a home, it can be hard work – both physically and emotionally. Don't be afraid of asking for help sometimes from your family and friends.

As a lone working parent, it's even more important for you than for other women to take care of your own wellbeing so that you can continue doing a good job of looking after your child. See Chapter 13 for a survival plan.

Christine Elliot, 32, is an administrator for a management consultancy in Leeds. Her four-year-old son, William, has just started primary school. Christine and her husband separated when William was nine months old.

It is difficult being on your own and working and being both mum and dad to your child. I have to make all the decisions, like choosing a school, and just hope I am doing the right thing.

But now that William is a bit older, I get more back from him than when he was a baby. He tells me about what he's done at school, which is nice.

Most of the time being a working mother is rewarding and I wouldn't change it for anything. At times I wish I could work part-time so I could spend more time with William. At weekends, although we have a lovely time together, I have to catch up on housework and I sometimes feel I don't give him enough.

I enjoy working. It gives me a sense of independence and I think I probably always will work. In an ideal world I would like to work for myself but I can't take that responsibility at the moment.

I enjoy the time after he's gone to bed – I stay up later now so I can have a little bit of time on my own. William sees his dad from time to time and I do like having peace and quiet at those times. And a friend baby-sits for William sometimes. I go out once a week on a Saturday night to keep my sanity and give me a break from being a mum.

I went back to work full-time when William was just twelve weeks old. It was hard going back so soon, but I didn't have a choice. You find yourself finishing work dead on time instead of staying an extra three-quarters of an hour. I definitely couldn't give as much as I used to at work. Your priorities change.

He went to a nursery until he was about 12 months old and then had a nanny for a year and a half. It sounds really posh but it was someone who had looked after him at the nursery, who had become a friend. She left the nursery and continued caring for him at the same rate I had been paying at the nursery.

The problem was that I couldn't claim any financial help with the cost through the tax-credit system. You are not eligible if someone is looking after your child on a private basis – only if you use a registered nursery or a registered child minder. Although the arrangement we had was all above board, my friend couldn't register as a child minder because she was looking after him in my home rather than her own. I wanted him to have consistent care, so I fought it – I wrote to my MP and everybody, took it as high as I could, saying, 'This is not fair'.

But in the end I had to tell my friend that I was going to have to send William to a nursery again. It almost ruined the relationship for a while, though it's fine again now. You feel you are not putting your child first, but I needed the extra money – it was a matter of survival.

At the new nursery, the fees were £540 a month but I got more than half of that back against my tax. The tax credit certainly made a difference. It made the nursery a lot more affordable.

Going from nursery to school is a big change. The nursery was open from eight in the morning till six-thirty at night, while school is from ten to nine until ten past three.

There is a breakfast club and an after-school club but I felt that if he went to both, I would never have any contact with the school and never see the teachers. I want to have a sense of how he is getting on in the classroom and I would never have that if I went on working the hours I was working – nine in the morning till five-thirty.

So I asked my boss if I could reduce my hours slightly and

take a pay cut. Now I drop William at school in the mornings and come into work for nine-thirty. William goes to the after-school club and I leave work at five in order to get back to pick him up when the club ends.

I have been with my company, Mercuri Urval, since William was two and a half. They have been fantastic to me – a lot of employers probably wouldn't have been as flexible as they have. I have had to take time off when William hurt himself at nursery and was rushed to casualty, and again when he had chickenpox.

William seems fine so far. I am sure there are going to be times when he says, 'Mummy, I want to go home with all my friends when their mummies pick them up after school.' I feel terrible. I'm not there, so I don't know what he goes through when he sees all his friends going home with their mummies and he gets taken round to the after-school club. It does make me wish I could pick him up every day but I know that is not possible.

But he is used to long days so it's not a sudden massive change for him. I'll just have to play it by ear and see how it goes – and maybe one day I will win the lottery or something!

My most difficult decision came when my marriage ended. With my husband I had moved up to Yorkshire from Worcestershire, where my parents live. We had been here in Yorkshire for twelve years and I felt that this was my home, but when we separated I had to decide whether to stay here or move back near my mum and dad.

I have good support here from friends, but you can ask a bit more from your family than you can from your friends.

My parents live in a small market town so if I had moved back I would have been able to earn only about half the salary

I am on now, but I would have had my mum to help me a lot more with William. It is one of the hardest decisions I've made and my mum probably still doesn't understand why I decided to stay in Yorkshire.

At first I rented various places but I have recently bought a house, so I feel settled again now.

The best thing about my life is seeing my little boy smile and tell me that he loves me. No matter how hard you work, what you do, what you can buy and what you've got in your house, I don't think there is anything better than the love you get from your child.

William is happy and that makes it all worthwhile.

Chapter 12:
Happy families

The idea of working mums spending 'quality time' with their children has gone out of fashion, and not before time. It's hardly fair to expect a child to want intense, high-quality interaction with you the minute you get in from work – he might be feeling tired or grumpy, or be in the middle of watching a television programme or playing on his computer.

'Quality time' with children is spontaneous – it can't be turned on at will or booked into the diary. Enjoy the moments of togetherness when they happen, but don't think you must have some 'quality time' every day, or you will feel bad when the reality falls short of your ideal.

The important thing is to be available for your child when he or she wants to talk, even if you are busy. You can't schedule it. There will be times when your child doesn't feel like talking to you, and other times when he does need to open up about something that's bothering him. Even if he doesn't want to talk, just being together, reading a story or cuddling on the sofa, can be a special time.

Out-of-school activities

We all know mums who feel they have to spend every spare minute improving their children – life is one long round of music lessons, cricket coaching, extra maths tuition, piano practice, ballet and karate. Most family conversations take place over mum's shoulder while the kids are in the back of the car en route to some activity or other.

No one in the family is allowed to relax and just 'be'. They might occasionally be allowed to read a book, provided it's educational, but sitting in front of the TV is seen as a cardinal sin.

There's even a name for it – 'schedule overload'. According to the experts, children who spend their lives going from one activity to the next may develop a lack of creative, organisational and decision-making skills, as well as lacking the motivation to succeed at things they really care about. Symptoms include signs of stress such as irritability, anxiety, worry, fatigue, apathy and loss of, or excessive, appetite.

Worried yet? You should be. Seriously, though, if you think that you and your children have been overdoing it a bit, it might be a good idea to ask yourself – and them – whether you would all benefit from cutting down on their organised activities.

Your quality of life will improve as you spend less time on frenzied cross-town journeys when you are all dog-tired and there's still a meal to organise and homework to be done. What's more, far from neglecting your parental duties and disadvantaging your child, you could be doing him a favour. Just like the rest of us, children need time to think, to use their imaginations, to relax. They need to be left alone sometimes so they have a chance to learn how to entertain themselves. They need to do their own thing – whatever that might be.

Saying no

One of the challenges of being a working mum is that it can be harder for us to say 'no' to our kids because we tend to feel, deep down, that we have to make it up to them for the fact that we go out to work.

If you haven't seen him all day, the last thing you want is your toddler throwing a tantrum or your child stomping off to his room to sulk because you've said 'no' to something he wants to do. Unfortunately though, unless we want our kids to grow up without any boundaries, parenting does involve saying no and being firm sometimes, even if it makes us feel wretched inside.

Carol says:

I try to keep a reality check on what my kids have – I don't want them to be spoiled just because we are lucky enough to be able to afford to buy them things.

Once, our children all got new bikes because they all needed a new one at the same time. We had a long chat with them about how this was a big deal and that normally they would have to wait until Christmas for something as special as this.

The next day Alex was away working when the three bikes arrived. And that day they were the most awful children I've ever clapped eyes on. I couldn't believe it. I had a huge barney with them.

So we took the bikes away and hid them. We told the kids they had gone back to the shop and that the man in the shop was going to keep them for a week, during which time they had to prove that they deserved to get the bikes back – otherwise they would be gone for good.

They were absolutely horrified. They cried themselves to sleep. It really put the wind up them. But you have got to prove you mean it – never make idle threats, or you'll be stuffed, they'll walk all over you!

It is one of the hardest things I have had to do. I was really upset but I explained: 'I could buy you new things but if things come too easily to you, you will not be a nice person. You have to understand that the bikes cost a lot of money and you blew it, big time.'

We kept the bikes away for a week and a half, and they were as good as gold.

Boy, did the message sink in. It was hard – but I'm pleased we did it.

Families under stress

No family is immune to problems. Money worries, illness, unemployment, bereavement and relationship difficulties can affect any of us.

Children are resilient and many cope amazingly well under difficult circumstances. But it's no good pretending that a stressed family life won't have any impact on children. How can we minimise the effects and help them through?

Anxiety and stress in children are not always obvious. Children might have difficulty in getting to sleep or have nightmares; they may have tummy upsets or start wetting the bed. They sometimes express emotional distress in rebellious or aggressive behaviour.

Children are sensitive to what happens around them. They may even feel that it is their fault when things go wrong.

They can feel anxious and insecure when they hear parents rowing or threatening to leave home. So, however bad things get in a relationship, it's important to protect children and, if humanly possible, save heated arguments for times when there's no danger they will overhear. We should never take our frustration and anger out on them – or expect them to provide support and a listening ear for us when we are faced with an unsympathetic partner.

When a crisis strikes

When life is busy and stressful, one more thing going wrong, like pranging the car, can tip the balance and make you feel that you just can't cope. But at times like this, your children need reassurance too.

Hearing a parent say, 'Oh my God, I can't cope with this, I'm leaving,' can be frightening for a child – you may not mean it, but your child doesn't know that.

The way you react to a crisis – whether it's a minor crisis or more serious – will affect the way your children feel and react, in

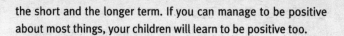

the short and the longer term. If you can manage to be positive about most things, your children will learn to be positive too.

At school

If something is happening at home that is troubling your child, have a word with his teacher so that he or she is aware of the situation and will understand why your child may be withdrawn or tearful at school.

Someone to talk to

Children who are going through stressful times shouldn't have to cope alone. But if things are difficult at home they can sometimes be reluctant to talk to their parents about their feelings.

Would your child find it easier to talk to someone else instead of you? Perhaps he could confide in granny or grandad or his teacher.

If your child is suffering emotional distress and you don't feel you can get him through it without help, ask your GP for a referral to a child psychologist, child psychotherapist or child guidance clinic.

Support from other parents

Bringing up kids can be difficult. *You* might need someone else to talk to as well. Parentline Plus is an organisation that offers help and information to parents and families. It runs Parent Network courses around the UK, where parents can meet for mutual support on the issues they are facing. It also runs a freephone helpline (see page 175).

Chapter 13:
Look after yourself

Life is supposed to be rosy once you've had a baby. You are meant to go from being a fulfilled and glowing new mum with a gorgeous baby to a career woman confidently balancing a rewarding job with a lovely home, a happy family and an active social life.

Call it the Superwoman syndrome, call it the myth of motherhood; the fact is that when our lives don't match up to these unrealistic expectations, it leaves many women feeling inadequate.

The Working Mum's Survival Plan

Mothers are notorious for putting everyone else's needs first. But there's a good reason why air stewardesses explaining what to do in the event of an emergency tell you to put the oxygen mask on yourself before putting one on your child.

Being a working mother is no different. You need to look after yourself so that you can look after your family and cope successfully with the challenge of balancing work and home life.

You know what you need? A survival plan.

Take time for yourself

'Me-time' is important for recharging your batteries and for reminding yourself that you are more than just a mother, a partner and an employee. It can be really difficult to carve out a bit of time for yourself – you can feel guilty about going out for an evening and leaving the kids again when you have been at work all day. But it is good for you – and if it helps you cope, it's good for everyone else in the family too.

Along with childcare commitments, domestic responsibilities and time for partners, many working parents don't feel they have enough 'me-time'. In a survey by the Chartered Institute of Personnel and Development in 2002, two-thirds of women interviewed said they didn't have enough time for themselves. Men are either better at making time for themselves or need less time, since only half of men interviewed felt they didn't have enough time to themselves.

Carol says:

When Christie was little I went to a sculpture evening class and it was the most exhilarating thing I'd done in ages. There was no pressure, I didn't need to be any good at it. I had two hours on a Monday night with no one judging how well or badly I was doing, just mucking about, getting my hands dirty and walking away from it after two hours, thinking: 'That was really good fun.' No children, no husband – just for me. I got so much out of it. Even if it's only for an hour a week, make it a priority to do something just for yourself. Even if you can't go out of the house, once the kids are in bed do something just for you. Now I do things like upholstery, sewing, sculpting and photography at home.

Suzanne says:

Soon after my twins were born I became very depressed. Guilt was one of the contributing factors – I felt guilty for wanting time to be me again. I kept going, ignoring what I was feeling until I broke down with exhaustion. With the support of my family and my doctor, I realised having time to myself would benefit me and my children. They love staying overnight with their grandparents once a week.

Ask for help

We all need a bit of help from other people sometimes. When you are feeling on top of things, help out your friends, for instance with baby-sitting or picking up their kids from school – they will return the favour when you are the one who needs a helping hand.

Carol says:

Never be afraid to admit that it's all got too much. Some people think they have to keep up the image that they're managing fine, but if you are finding it a strain I think you have to call on your family and friends. People are willing to help – maybe not on a long-term basis, but just in the short term to help you through the tricky bits.

Cherish your friends

Friends help us celebrate our successes and, when things go wrong, help us pick ourselves up and start over. They help us get things back in perspective when we are worried and allow us to let off steam when we're mad.

Carol says:

Sometimes you arrange a night out with girlfriends and when the evening comes round you think: 'I'm so tired, I could do without this.' But you go, you have a great time and

⊙ Getting out of a boring job into something more stimulating.

⊙ Getting out of a stressful job into something less demanding.

⊙ Having more time to yourself.

⊙ Spending more time with your child.

⊙ Looking after your child yourself instead of using childcare.

What are your options?

You could:

⊙ Spend some money on a cleaner and someone to do the ironing, to give yourself more time to do the things you want to do.

⊙ Pay your child minder to work another few hours a week, over and above the time you are working, to give you some time to yourself.

⊙ Look into the possibility of working part-time in your current job.

⊙ Give up your current job and find another way to earn enough money to get by.

⊙ If you have a partner, give up your job and reduce your outgoings enough to allow you to manage on his wages alone.

Aruni de Silva and her husband Suvendra live in north London and have two children – six-year-old Bishata and five-year-old Sachin. Aruni, who comes from Sri Lanka, is an accountant.

I was an accountant with a charity when I had Bishata. I had to go back to work – if I hadn't, we couldn't have made ends meet.

For the first three months that I was back at work, my mum, who lives in Sri Lanka, was staying with me. But when Bishata was eight months old my mum went back to Sri Lanka and I had to find a child minder.

I tried four child minders but they all said, after two or three days, that they couldn't keep her because she cried so much. I had to take a lot of time off work during this period – I would sit in my car outside their house, listening to her and crying myself.

I felt I couldn't leave Bishata like that – so I decided I had to leave my job. But the organisation I worked for wouldn't accept my resignation – they told me to take a bit more time off to sort it out.

As a last resort I found an older lady who would come to our house to look after her and luckily Bishata took to her straight away. This lady was also from Sri Lanka, so perhaps Bishata thought that it was my mum who had come back. She wasn't qualified but she had had children and grandchildren of her own and she was very good with Bishata – it was a massive relief.

When Bishata was fourteen months old, I had my son. When I went back after my maternity leave, Bishata went to a nursery three days a week and this lady continued to come to our house to look after Sachin.

But she wasn't very reliable and one Friday she told me that she wouldn't be coming any more – she had found another job that paid more. I was livid – I said, 'They are kids, not animals, and you can't just dump them like that.'

Anyway, I spent the weekend phoning everyone I could think of to find someone else who would be able to look after Bishata and Sachin. Even if I was going to have to leave my job, I had to work my notice.

My husband took a week off and I found another Sri Lankan lady who could look after Sachin from the following week. Bishata went to the nursery full-time.

After a while I changed jobs and moved to a company in the private sector. I needed someone more reliable so I put both children in a private nursery. It was easier because even if someone is unwell, there are other staff there. However, it was very expensive.

I would drop the children off in the morning and pick them up after work. They continued at the nursery until they started school.

My company relocated and for a while I was dropping Bishata and Sachin off at another parent's house at eight in the morning and driving fifty miles to work. It was exhausting.

I realised I would have to find a job that was nearer home, that offered more support for working mothers. I got a local job in the voluntary sector as a community accountant, advising charities on their finances.

At first my husband, who is an IT consultant, could pick the children up from school because he started work at 6 a.m. and finished at 2 p.m. But earlier this year he was made redundant so he is now self-employed and he needs to put in longer hours. We have had to cut down a lot – mine is the main salary now.

I have asked my present employers if I can work flexitime so that I can start at 7.30 a.m. and leave at 3 p.m. to pick the children up from school. That would also allow me to take them to their activities – ballet, football and swimming. If the answer is no, I will have to find a child minder to collect them from school – but a child minder wouldn't be able to take them to their activities.

It has been difficult – it was sink or swim at times and I have felt guilty about leaving the children. I am mentally very strong so I was able to cope – but I can see why some people can't.

During the week I turn a blind eye to the housework. At least there is food on the table at the end of the day! My husband cooks, but he doesn't like to clean, so some weekends I spend a lot of time catching up on housework.

I do enjoy my work and I have invested so much time and money into training as an accountant that I didn't want to give up. And I like exercising my brain cells. In my profession, if I had stayed at home for five years it would be very difficult to get back – there are so many changes in IT, legislation and work practice. But if I could work from home or become a consultant, I would take that option.

Don't make rash decisions

When there are problems at work or at home that are making your life hell, it can be tempting to put a quick end to the misery by resigning. But even if you long for the satisfaction of telling your boss where to stick his job, don't make any rash decisions on something as important as this.

You may be able to work through some temporary problems, for instance by taking parental leave to cope with a childcare emergency.

If you are thinking of handing in your notice, first work out what you really want and the best way to get it.

Beware the 'grass is greener' syndrome. Being at home won't necessarily be the answer to all your problems – you may simply find you have different problems! Go back to square one and think through all the issues again to remind yourself of why you chose to go back to work in the first place and what the good things are about work (there might be some!).

Can you afford to give up?

If you definitely want to make changes, work out whether you could afford to go part-time, reduce your hours or even give up altogether.

To find out you need to go through the budgeting exercise in Chapter 9, if you haven't already. This will tell you whether your partner's current salary alone would meet your family's needs and, if there is a shortfall, how serious it is. Can you pay off your debts on one salary? If one salary meets your day-to-day needs, how important is it for you to save for the future?

Going down the list, you will see that the things towards the end of the list are those that make life that bit more fun. But the point is that you could do without them if you had to. Work out which little luxuries you would both be prepared to give up.

If you gave up work you wouldn't have any childcare costs, of course. You'd also spend less on things like commuting and buying clothes for work.

Now add up the sums again. Could you manage? Look at the other suggestions for saving money, such as moving your mortgage. Or does the situation call for more desperate measures?

If you have a partner, the two of you need to sit down together and work out whether giving up work is a real option for you. How would your partner feel about the pressure of being the sole breadwinner? How secure is his job? How would you feel about being financially dependent on him?

If there is a major shortfall, managing on one income could involve big changes in your lifestyle and a radical reassessment of your long-term plans. But if being away from your child is making you really miserable and you would do anything to give up work, you might be motivated enough to accept these changes.

For some families this might mean simply giving up plans to send their child to a private school or doing without a second car. For others, it could mean giving up the family car, the summer holiday, maybe even moving to a smaller house or relocating to an area where property and the cost of living are cheaper. Ouch! But this could still be the solution that brings you peace of mind and makes you feel richer in the things that really matter.

Chapter 14:
Your rights at work

The bottom line

This section outlines the minimum standards that you, as an employed pregnant woman or working parent, are entitled to by law. You may be lucky enough to work for an organisation that offers much better maternity or parental-leave arrangements than these – but no employer is allowed to offer arrangements which do not meet these minimum government standards. Always check to see if your own organisation has an agreement that offers a better deal.

Check out the details

In the space available here we can only give you a guide to your employment rights – for more detailed advice on your own situation, you'll need to seek out further information and we tell you where you can find this.

Some of the amounts, such as child benefit rates, are liable to be altered each April in the Budget and employment rights do change from time to time, so you'll need to check out the situation as it applies to you.

Are you an employee?

The rights apply to part-time workers as well as full-time workers, no matter how many hours they work, provided they satisfy any qualifying conditions such as length of service. However, if you are self-employed or unemployed, much of this section will not apply to you (though you may be entitled to Maternity Allowance, see below). And surprisingly, for women in the police force, the rights relating to time off for antenatal care, maternity leave, parental leave and protection against unfair dismissal in connection with maternity leave don't apply.

Time off for antenatal care

If you are pregnant and an employee, you are entitled to paid time off for antenatal care. That includes relaxation and parent-craft classes, if these are held during your work time, as well as things like clinic visits and ultrasound scans. You're entitled to this time off, regardless of how long you have been with your employer.

What you have to do

Except in the case of your first appointment, you have to show your employer on request:

⊙ A certificate from your doctor, midwife or health visitor confirming that you are pregnant.

⊙ The appointment card showing the date and time of your appointment.

Maternity leave

Who's entitled to maternity leave?

⊙ You are entitled to 26 weeks of Ordinary Maternity Leave (OML), regardless of how long you have been with your employer. (For how much money you will get during this period, see below.)

⊙ You are entitled to Additional Maternity Leave (AML) if you have completed 26 weeks' service with your employer by the 15th week before the week that the baby is due. This additional leave is for a further 26 weeks, starting from the end of OML. It is unpaid (unless your organisation has other arrangements).

What happens to your employment contract?

⊙ During both types of maternity leave, your contract of

employment continues – unless either you or your employer
ends it or unless it would have expired anyway.

⊙ While you are on OML, all the terms and conditions relating
to your employment continue, for instance your holiday
entitlement will continue to accrue – the big exception is your
wages or salary. But see the section on Maternity Pay, below.

⊙ The time that you are on AML counts towards your period of
continuous employment only for certain entitlements. For
instance, unlike the OML period, your employer does not
have to count the AML period for the purpose of assessing
seniority, pension rights and other payments based on your
length of service. As already pointed out, some employers
agree contracts of employment providing better terms – but
if yours hasn't, the period of employment before the start of
your AML will be 'joined up' with your return to work as if they
were a continuous period of employment.

Compulsory maternity leave

Just in case you are one of those superwomen who is itching to
get back to the boardroom the minute the umbilical cord has
been cut, let me break it to you gently: there is also something
called Compulsory Maternity Leave. You must take leave for two
weeks after your baby is born – and if you work in a factory, this is
extended to four weeks.

When can maternity leave start?

No earlier than the eleventh week before the week your baby is
due. But if you prefer to have as much of it as possible after your
baby is born, you can even continue working right up until the
baby arrives, if you can manage it!

What's the most leave could you get?

If you are entitled just to OML, you'll get 26 weeks. If you're entitled to AML as well, it's a total of 52 weeks.

If for some reason you need more time before you go back to work, you could consider taking up to four weeks' Parental Leave too – see below.

Maternity leave: what you have to do

⊙ You have to notify your employer by the 'notification week' (the fifteenth week before the week that the baby is due), that you are pregnant, your due date and when you want your leave to start. If you want to make any changes to this later, you must give four weeks' notice.

⊙ If you decide to leave while you are on OML or AML, you must give your employer the right length of notice (as set out in your employment contract), just as you would have done if you were handing in your notice at any other time.

You will find a useful Maternity Leave Plan (a simple form you can use to notify your employer) on the Department of Trade and Industry website www.tiger.gov.uk

Maternity pay or allowance

Some employers have more generous schemes, but the minimum you are entitled to is this:

⊙ Statutory Maternity Pay (SMP) is paid by your employer for 26 weeks, provided you meet the qualifying conditions based on your length of service and average earnings.

⊙ SMP is paid at 90 per cent of your salary for the first six weeks and a flat rate for the remaining period (in 2006–7 the rate is £108.85 a week – or 90 per cent of your earnings if this is less than £108.85 a week).

⊙ Most of this is reimbursed to your employer by the government.

⊙ Even if you don't qualify for SMP you may qualify for Maternity

Allowance (MA, see below), which is paid by your local Jobcentre Plus or social security office.

⊙ You only get SMP or MA for weeks in which you are not working.

Who gets SMP?

You get SMP if you are pregnant or have just given birth and:

⊙ You have worked for your employer continuously for at least 26 weeks before the qualifying week, which is the 15th week before the week in which your baby is due. Your average weekly earnings in the eight weeks up to and including this qualifying week must have been high enough to be relevant for National Insurance purposes (you don't necessarily have to have been paying NI contributions though). This limit changes every year and is around £84 a week.

⊙ If you qualify, you get SMP whether or not you are intending to return to your job.

What you have to do to get SMP

⊙ Tell your employer that you intend to stop work to have a baby – you must give notice by the qualifying week (see above).

⊙ Give your employer medical evidence of the date your baby is due. This will normally be on a maternity certificate (MATB1) that you can get from your doctor or midwife twenty weeks (or less) before the baby is due. You should give your employer the medical evidence no later than three weeks after the date SMP was due to start.

More than one employer?

If you work for more than one employer, you may be entitled to SMP from each one. You can stop work with each employer at different times if it suits you – your maternity pay periods can start at different times with each employer.

Who gets Maternity Allowance?

You can claim MA if:

⊙ You are employed but not eligible for SMP.

⊙ You have been employed or self-employed for (get your diary out) at least 26 weeks of the 66-week period ending with the week before your baby is due.

⊙ You pass the earnings test – you must have earned over a certain set amount in a 13-week 'test period'.

How much is MA?

MA is paid at £108.85 per week (for 2006–7), or 90 per cent of your average earnings, depending on how much you earn.

How long is it paid for?

It is paid for 26 weeks. If you are employed or self-employed, you choose the week when you want it to start – this week must be no earlier than the 11th week before the week your baby is due.

What you have to do

Claim using form MA1, which you can get from your antenatal clinic or the Benefits Agency.

How is it paid?

By an order book, which you can cash weekly at a post office, or it can be paid directly into your bank or building society account every four weeks.

What if you are ill?

⊙ You will normally be able to take sick leave until you start your maternity leave on the date you have notified. If the illness is unrelated to your pregnancy you can remain on sick leave and receive Statutory Sick Pay or Incapacity Benefit right up to the date your leave starts.

⊙ If the illness is pregnancy-related and you are in the last four weeks of pregnancy, your maternity-leave period will be triggered automatically on the first day you are absent from work. To protect your rights, you have to tell your employer that you are away from work wholly or partly because of your pregnancy, as soon as is 'reasonably practicable'.

Going back to work

If you decide to go back to work before the end of your OML or AML, you have to give your employer at least four weeks' notice of the date of your return. (This does not have to be in writing.)

You don't have to give notice if you are simply returning to work immediately after the end of your maternity leave.

See Chapter 3 for tips on managing your return to work.

Do you get your old job back?

When you go back to work after either OML or AML, you are entitled to return to the same job on the same terms and conditions, unless a redundancy situation has arisen.

If a redundancy situation has arisen, you are entitled to be offered a suitable alternative vacancy.

After AML, if there is some reason other than redundancy why it is not 'reasonably practicable' for you to have your old job back, you should be offered a similar job. The work should be 'suitable and appropriate' and the capacity and place in which you are to be employed and the status and terms and conditions should be no less favourable than in your old job.

There are some exceptions to this rule, however: it does not necessarily apply where a firm employs five or fewer employees, or where your job has become redundant and your employer can show that there is no suitable alternative work to offer you.

If the offer is 'suitable' and you turn it down, you are considered to have resigned. If you don't believe it is suitable, you could bring a complaint of unfair dismissal to an employment tribunal (see Problems, below).

Your employer is not allowed to impose less favourable terms and conditions on you when you resume work after maternity leave. If yours tries this on, seek professional help, perhaps from a law centre, Citizens' Advice Bureau or your trade union. Working Families can advise you (see page 177). You may decide to take your employer to court claiming damages for breach of contract or to resign and make a complaint of constructive unfair dismissal to an employment tribunal.

Health and safety

Some kinds of work are hazardous in pregnancy or to breast-feeding mothers – for instance jobs involving certain chemical agents, processes and working conditions. Employers are required by law to assess risks in the workplace to these groups of women and their babies and to take measures to prevent exposure to the risks if these could damage the health or safety of a pregnant woman or new mother and her baby.

These risks include things like regular exposure to shocks, vibration or movement; manual handling of loads where there is a risk of injury; physical demands of the job such as standing all day or working at heights; or exposure to radiation and certain biological and chemical agents. Official advice also warns against working in compressed air and underwater diving. But if you are concerned about working with a VDU, the government does not consider this to pose a risk and says that no special protective measures are needed.

Where there is deemed to be a risk:

⊙ Your working conditions must be adjusted or, if this is not reasonable or would not avoid the risk, you must be offered suitable alternative work if there is any. If there isn't, you can be suspended from work on maternity grounds. You must be paid your normal wages for as long as the suspension lasts, and your employer cannot dismiss you because of this.

⊙ You must not be required to work at night if you have a medical certificate stating that night work could damage your health or safety. If there is no suitable daytime work to offer you, you may be suspended from work, on full pay, for as long as necessary.

⊙ These rights apply regardless of your length of service or hours of work.

⊙ If you think your work involves a risk to your (or your baby's) health and safety, which your employer has not considered or won't act on, you should bring it to your employer's attention or notify your workplace health and safety representative.

⊙ If this doesn't get you anywhere, contact your local office of the Health and Safety Executive for advice.

Paternity leave

Dads who are eligible will be able to take up to two weeks' leave (see Chapter Ten, page 118) paid at the same rate as Statutory Maternity Pay – currently £108.85 a week or 90 per cent of average earnings if this is less.

Adoptive parents

Adoptive parents are entitled to adoption leave and pay and paternity leave and pay, as well as parental leave (see below).

Parental leave

You are entitled to parental leave if you are the mother or father of a child under five and have completed one year's service with your employer by the time you want to take the leave. This is a type of leave, usually unpaid, which allows mothers and fathers time off work to look after a child or make arrangements for the child's welfare.

Each parent can take a total of 13 weeks' parental leave in the first five years of a child's life. (Parents of disabled children are entitled to 18 weeks' leave to be taken at any time up to the child's 18th birthday.) You can take it in blocks of between one and four weeks.

Examples of the way the leave might be used include:

⊙ Spending more time with your child in the early years.

⊙ Staying with your child when he or she is in hospital.

⊙ Checking out schools.

⊙ Settling a child into new childcare arrangements.

How much notice is required?

Normally an employee has to give at least 21 days' notice to the employer of the dates the parental leave will start and finish (though some employers may be more flexible than this).

However, if an employer thinks that the employee's absence would unduly disrupt the business, he can postpone the leave and must tell the employee within seven days of the reason for the postponement and the new dates.

Your employer is not allowed to dismiss or discriminate against you because you want to take parental leave.

Time off for dependants

Because of the requirement to give notice, parental leave is not very useful in terms of looking after a sick child (or if your child minder is sick, for instance). However, you are also entitled to take time off to look after dependants in certain cases.

All employees have the right to unpaid time off to deal with emergencies involving someone who is dependent on them. There is no set amount of time – it depends on the circumstances. The official guidance says you can take 'what is reasonable to make arrangements for the care of the dependant'.

Flexible working hours

If you are the parent of a child under six or a disabled child under eighteen you may request a more flexible working pattern and your employer has a legal duty to consider this properly.

You must submit a written application, setting out the changes you would like (see 'Asking for change', page 22). Guidance is available on how to go about this – contact the Department of Trade and Industry (contact details on page 168).

Problems

If you want to complain because you feel that your employment rights have been infringed, the first step is, of course, to try and sort it out with your employer. If informal approaches don't produce a result, you might have to go through your organisation's grievance or appeals procedure. (If you haven't tried this first, any compensation that an employment tribunal might award you at a later date could be reduced.)

You need to act quickly because normally you have to complain to an employment tribunal within three months of the date on which the problem occurred, for instance the date you were refused time off for an antenatal appointment or the date on which you were unfairly dismissed.

Maternity pay disputes

Disputes about maternity benefit entitlement are not dealt with by employment tribunals. Contact the Department for Work and Pensions or the Inland Revenue to find out what to do in these cases.

If your employer says you are not entitled to SMP or pays you less than you think you are entitled to, ask for an explanation. They must give you form SMP1, stating the reasons. If you think your employer's decision is wrong, you can ask for advice from your local Inland Revenue (NI Contributions) office or from your trade union or staff association. If necessary, the Inland Revenue will look at the evidence in writing from you and your employer and make a formal decision.

(If you are not entitled to SMP, you may be able to get MA – complete form MA1 from your social security office or maternity clinic and send it with form SMP1 and your maternity certificate, to you social security office.)

Redundancy

If your employer is making redundancies and he wants to choose you for redundancy during your maternity leave, he must comply with certain requirements: he must offer you a suitable alternative vacancy either within the same organisation or with an associated employer.

If there is a suitable alternative vacancy but your employer doesn't offer it to you, the redundancy will be regarded as an unfair dismissal.

However, if he offers it to you and you turn it down 'unreasonably', you may forfeit your right to a redundancy payment.

Sex discrimination

Women who are pregnant, have recently given birth or are breast-feeding may have certain extra protections under the Sex Discrimination Act 1975. This says that women must not be discriminated against directly or indirectly on the grounds of sex or marriage.

Indirect sex discrimination occurs where an employer applies a condition or requirement that fewer women than men would be able to comply with.

If you believe you have been discriminated against on the grounds of sex or marriage, you can complain to an employment tribunal.

How to complain to an employment tribunal

Contact your local employment service Jobcentre or phone the DTI publications order line on 0870 1502 500 and request a copy of the booklet *How to apply to an employment tribunal*.

The employment tribunal office will send a copy of your completed complaint form to a conciliator of the Advisory, Conciliation and Arbitration Service (ACAS), who will attempt to get you and your employer to settle the problem.

If that can't be done an employment tribunal will hear your case, and both you and your employer will attend. If the tribunal rules in your favour it can order the employer to reinstate you in your job, re-engage you in a similar one or, if you don't want to go back, make a cash award for compensation.

Do you want to make a difference?

If you feel passionately about maternity rights, child care provision, or working parents' need to achieve work-life balance, you could get involved with one of the organisations which campaign, lobby and raise awareness on these issues among the public, employers and government. By adding your voice to the work done by organisations such as Working Families (see page 177) and the Daycare Trust (see page 170), you could help to change things for other working parents.

Further information

Association for Postnatal Illness
145 Dawes Road
Fulham
London
SW6 7EB
Helpline: 020 7386 0868
Website: www.apni.org.uk

Information available on the website or by post (enclose SAE); a network of telephone volunteers, who have themselves experienced postnatal illness, to support women suffering from this condition.

British Franchise Association
Thames View
Newtown Road
Henley on Thames
Oxfordshire
RG9 1HG
Tel: 01491 578050
E-mail: mailroom@thebfa.org
Website: www.thebfa.org

Advice on choosing a franchise, seminars and publications.

Children's Information Service
To find your local CIS, which can give you information about childcare where you live, call Childcare Link on 08000 96 02 96 or see the website at www.childcarelink.gov.uk.

Daycare Trust
21 St George's Road
London
SE1 6ES
Tel: 020 7840 3350
E-mail: info@daycaretrust.org.uk
Website: www.daycaretrust.org.uk

Direct Selling Association
29 Floral Street
London
WC2E 9DP
Tel: 020 7497 1234
Website: www.dsa.org.uk

Information about direct-selling opportunities.

Flexecutive
Shropshire House
179 Tottenham Court Road
London
W1T 7NZ
Tel: 020 7636 6744
E-mail: general@flexecutive.co.uk
Website: www.flexecutive.co.uk

A recruitment company that helps experienced and qualified people to find flexible employment in marketing, human
resources, finance and IT. It runs a national job-share register
to help people looking for a job-share partner, especially in
teaching. It also runs workshops to help flexible workers work
effectively together.

Gingerbread
307 Borough High Street
London
SE1 1JH
Tel: 020 7403 9500
Advice line: Freephone 0800 018 4318
E-mail: office@gingerbread.org.uk
Website: www.gingerbread.org.uk

Network of local self-help and support groups for lone parents in England and Wales, plus information and publications and an e-mail discussion list.

Gingerbread Scotland
1014 Argyle Street
Glasgow
G3 8LX
Tel: 0141 576 5085/7976

Gingerbread Northern Ireland
169 University Street
Belfast
BT7 1HR
Northern Ireland
Tel: 028 90 231 417
Website: www.gingerbreadni.org

La Leche League (Great Britain)
PO Box 29
West Bridgford
Nottingham
NG2 7NP
24-hour helpline: 0845 120 2918
Website: www.laleche.org.uk
Books online: www.lllbooks.org.uk

Organisation for breast-feeding mothers. Local groups have monthly meetings where you can meet other mothers, discuss various topics including working and breast-feeding, hire a breast pump or borrow books. Also, volunteers offer one-to-one support and encouragement.

Learndirect
Freepost
York House
Manchester
M2 9RU
Tel: freephone 0800 101901 (lines are open between 8 a.m. and 10 p.m.)
Scotland: 0800 100900
Website: www.learndirect.org.uk

An on-line learning network offering over 650 courses and free, impartial information and advice on a huge range of courses nationwide. Some Learndirect courses are free, many are subsidised by the government. You can learn at home, at one of the 1,700 centres or anywhere you have access to the Internet.

Maternity benefits
Phone the Department for Work and Pensions on 020 7712 2171. They will tell you the phone number of your local DSS Office (Benefits Agency). Or look up Benefits Agency in your local phone directory.

National Childbirth Trust
Alexandra House
Oldham Terrace
Acton
London
W3 6NH
Tel: 0870 770 3236
Enquiry line: 0870 444 8707
Membership: 0870 990 8040
Breast-feeding: 0870 444 8708
Website: www.nct.org.uk

Antenatal classes; support groups for new mothers; events such as coffee mornings, nearly-new sales and baby massage; breast-feeding counsellors; and a 'special experiences register' of mothers who have come through difficult times who can share what they have learned and listen if you need to talk.

National Childminding Association
Royal Court
81 Tweedy Road
Bromley
Kent
BR1 1TG
Free advice and information line for child minders and parents, Monday – Friday, 10 a.m. – 4 p.m: 0800 169 4486
Website: www.ncma.org.uk

Membership organisation for child minders; information for anyone in England thinking of becoming a child minder; advice for parents, including a free booklet on choosing a child minder.

Information for people outside England is available from the following organisations:

Wales: National Care Standards Inspectorate: 01443 848 450

Scotland: Care Commission: 0845 603 0890

Northern Ireland: Northern Ireland Childminding Association: 028 9181 1015

National Council for One Parent Families
255 Kentish Town Road
London
NW5 2LX
Telephone: 020 7428 5400
Fax: 020 7482 4851
Lone Parent Helpline: 0800 018 5026
E-mail: info@oneparentfamilies.org.uk
Website: www@oneparentfamilies.org.uk

Information for people bringing up children on their own; advice on maintenance, benefits and other money matters is available on the helpline

National Day Nurseries Association
Oak House
Woodvale Road
Brighouse
West Yorkshire
HD6 4AB
Tel: 0870 7744244
Website: www.ndna.org.uk

You can request a list of NDNA members and a booklet on what to ask when you look at nurseries.

New Ways to Work
26 Shacklewell Lane
Dalston
London
E8 2EZ
Helpline: 020 7503 3578
E-mail: information@new-ways.co.uk
Website: www.new-ways.co.uk

Advice on flexible and family-friendly working arrangements, including how to negotiate a different package with your employer. Free information pack and helpline.

One Parent Families Scotland
13 Gayfield Square
Edinburgh
EH1 3NX
Tel: 0131 556 3899
Website: opfs.org.uk

Parental leave, maternity rights at work and working time regulations
For further information see direct.gov.uk.

Parentline Plus
520 Highgate Studios
53–79 Highgate Road
Kentish Town
London
NW5 1TL
Tel: 020 7284 5500.
Helpline: 0808 8002222
Website: www.parentlineplus.org.uk

Help and information for parents and families; courses held around the UK, where parents can meet for mutual support; also a freephone helpline.

Professional Association of Nursery Nurses (PANN)
2 St James Court
Friar Gate
Derby
DE1 1BT
01332 372337
www.pat.org.uk

Union for child carers and part of the Professional Association of Teachers (PAT), PANN publishes an information pack on employing a nanny.

Relate

To find your local branch of Relate, look in your telephone directory or visit the website www.relate.org.uk (in Scotland, visit www.couplecounselling.org).

To talk to someone or to find out if counselling could help you, call Relate on 0845 456 1310.

Relate Direct is a new telephone counselling service that allows you to arrange counselling sessions over the phone at a time that suits you. This costs £30 to £45 per hour. Call Relate's central booking line on 0845 1 30 40 16 (Monday to Friday 9.30 a.m. to 4.30 p.m.).

Tax Credit Hotline

For information on tax credits or a claim form, phone 0845 300 3900, or claim on line via the website www.taxcredits.inlandrevenue.gov.uk.

Women Returners Network
Chelmsford College
Moulsham Street
Chelmsford
Essex
CM2 0JQ
Tel: 01245 263796
E-mail: womenreturners@hotmail.com
Website: www.women-returners.co.uk

Advice on courses for women returners. A workbook to help you identify your skills and start your job search is available for £5.

Working Families
1–3 Berry Street
London
EC1V 0AA
Tel: 020 7253 7243
Website: workingfamilies.org.uk

INDEX

you think: 'This is really nice.' I've got two or three close girl-friends that I keep up with.

I have friends who are working mothers and I find that listening to how they handle things helps me. With some of life's problems, it isn't always about having the money to do it – it's having the willpower. The willpower to say, 'Right, I'm not going to do this any more and I'm going to spend more time doing that,' or to be firm with the children about something.

If none of your friends has children and you want to meet other mums for friendship and support, you could contact an organisation like the National Childbirth Trust, which has local groups. You could arrange a reunion of your antenatal group or, if you work in a large organisation, you could even organise a parents' support group there.

Be your own best friend

You need to be your own best friend too. Many of us have a little voice in our head that says things like 'you're not good enough' or 'you've made a mess of things'. We demoralise ourselves by focusing on setbacks and any minor criticism, instead of thinking, 'Ninety-nine times out of a hundred my boss is happy.'

Instead of negative thinking, we can learn to give ourselves more positive messages – the kind of thing we would do for any of our friends. Make an effort to replace your negative thoughts with a more positive outlook, and it will gradually make a difference.

If you find yourself afraid to make a decision in case it's the wrong one, ask yourself: 'What's the worst that can happen?'

Make use of mental techniques like 'creative visualisation' – for instance, imagine you are outside in a summer shower and all your worries are being washed away.

Tell yourself things will get better

When you are going through a nightmare time – your baby won't sleep during the hours of darkness, your toddler is turning into a little dictator, the whole family has nits or your house has been burgled – remind yourself that all things pass. The challenges facing you at the moment will probably be but a distant memory by this time next year!

Carol says:

By the time you have your third child you recognise the signs and think: 'I know what this is, I know how to deal with it and it won't last long.' At times, as a mother, you feel you are wishing their lives away. You say: 'It will be easier when she can sit up,' or 'It will be easier when he can walk.' And then when they are walking, and they are into everything, you think: 'Why wasn't I happy when I could lie them down in one place and they would still be there when I came back?'

Learn how to let go of stress

Being able to completely relax your body and mind makes a big difference to the way you feel. Unconsciously you may be spending a lot of your day in 'fight or flight' mode and experiencing the physiological changes that produce symptoms of stress. Make time, somehow, for a class (such as yoga, transcendental meditation or relaxation therapy) that will teach you techniques to deepen your breathing, slow down your heartbeat and release all the stress and tension.

Don't take on too much

Often we take on more than we can comfortably manage, life becomes increasingly hectic and we end up exhausted and stressed. (That includes your children's activities as well as your work and other commitments.) Be realistic about how much you can cope with and don't overcommit yourself.

Try not to be a perfectionist – you put yourself under unnecessary pressure if everything always has to be perfect.

When you are struggling, call in reinforcements – your mum, your friends, your neighbour. Ask someone to take the kids off your hands for a while, and cancel anything that you don't actually have to do.

Postnatal depression

Giving birth causes huge and sudden changes in your body's hormonal balance. This, combined with the tiredness and the life changes that result from having a baby, can sometimes trigger postnatal depression.

This is not the same as the 'baby blues', that period just after the birth when you burst into tears at the drop of a hat. It can take two forms – in the first, rather than going away after a few days, the 'baby blues' persists and gets worse. In the second, postnatal illness develops weeks or months after the birth.

A woman suffering from postnatal illness becomes depressed, sad, anxious or unable to concentrate. She may lack energy, suffer from loss of appetite, insomnia, perhaps even panic attacks and suicidal feelings. She may be afraid that she does not love her baby. It can be hard to function at all, even to look after herself or the baby.

Anyone can be affected – rich or poor, married or single, first-time mum or not. Often they are women who seem to have everything going for them.

Women suffering from postnatal depression often feel guilty and ashamed – they think, 'I have got everything I wanted, why aren't I happy?' But if you suffer from postnatal depression, it is important to remember that it is not your fault. And you *will* get better.

You need to talk to the people closest to you about how you

are feeling. Talk to your health visitor or doctor too. It is important to get enough rest and sleep, because exhaustion makes things much worse. You also need support, reassurance and understanding from the people around you. In some cases, women also need antidepressants to help them recover.

Sometimes it can help to talk to someone else who has been through a similar experience and come out the other side. The Association for Postnatal Illness (see contact details on page 169) has a network of volunteers who have themselves experienced this condition, who will support women by telephone or mail to help them through it and give them hope and reassurance.

Some women who suffer from postnatal depression during their maternity leave cannot imagine feeling well enough to go back to work. Others manage to return and find that being back at work actually helps their depression to lift.

If your Ordinary Maternity Leave is over and you need longer to recover before you go back, you may be able to take Additional Maternity Leave (if you are entitled to it) or sick leave, or any annual leave owed to you, or parental leave (or a combination of these).

You may be able to get Statutory Sick Pay while you are on Additional Maternity Leave as long as you claim it straight after your Ordinary Maternity Leave. You will not be able to receive it if you claim it at the end of your AML because you have to be earning in the weeks before you make the claim.

When times get tough

Perhaps you went back to your job but you are not enjoying it and have found it too stressful to combine motherhood and full-time work. Perhaps your child is not happy in childcare, you can't find any suitable alternative and you want to stay at home with him instead. Or perhaps you are simply fed up with your job.

Think about your situation and work out what is making you unhappy and what is your greatest priority. This might be: